The
Redrock Canyon
Explorer

A Virtual Visit To
An Imaginary Canyon

written and illustrated
by
Irene Brady

The Explorer Library

Nature Works
2000

This book is dedicated to my best friend and husband, Daniel.

and in memory of Dave Siddon
and for Wildlife Images Rehabilitation Center — where wildlife gets a second chance.

Many people have helped in the concept, preparation, writing and illustration of this book. In fact, I have an amazingly talented matrix of family, friends and colleagues. Daniel, my dear husband, has offered unstinting support throughout its long gestation and hatching. He helped me plan its format, edited text, suggested illustrations and made my research trips possible. His support, sense of wonder, and joy of life are among my most valuable resources.

My sister, Diane Harris, lives in the redrock country of this book. I've climbed her mesas, explored with her the caves and potholes, visited ancient Puebloan (also known as Anasazi) dwellings, and marveled over the life to be found in its magical secret places. She gave me lodging in her beautiful FireTree Bed & Breakfast guest hogan (see at www.natureworksbooks.com/firetree.html), suggested research references, then diligently and expertly edited this book for grammatical, anecdotal and scientific accuracy. Several times.

Sharon Brussels and Steve Grah at Canyonlands Natural History Association gave me encouragement and marketing tips and suggested a page on alien invaders (plants and animals, that is!). Donna Budd-Jack and Linda Martin at Mesa Verde advised me on American Indian matters. Dr. William H. "Terry" Wright, Professor of Geology, Sonoma State University, and Dr. Margaret N. Rees, Professor of Geology, University of Nevada at Las Vegas, provided geological information. Loyd Berry of the Colorado Weed Management Association gave botanical assistance on aliens. Steve Siewert shared his Arizona desert expertise and insight, and lent me research materials.

My brother, David Brady, provided invaluable computer hardware and software training and support, and advised me on printing matters, as well as producing terrific printed promotional materials and assisting in the final edit. My nephew, Ben Brady, proofed the manuscript from a pre-teen vantage point. My sister, Laura O'Brady, and my late friend, Nelda Lewis, helped with copy-proofing. Sharon Heisel did a herculean job of scientific and grammatical editing. Marcia Way-Brady, my sister-in-law, assisted with editing on the final round. Dr. Stephen Cross, Professor of Biology at Southern Oregon University, advised me on reptilian scientific nomenclature. Darby Morrell offered invaluable insight on format and many other matters, checked for continuity, and worked on the final edit. Drs. Ronald Lamb (biology) and Frank Lang (botany), Professors Emeritus, Department of Biology at Southern Oregon University, also polished the final edit with useful observations. Uncle Dave Luman provided research materials and suggested changes in the manuscript. Ron and Pat Ashley provided last minute encouragement. Any errors are entirely my responsibility.

But I might not have started the project at all without the last promise I made my friend Dave Siddon, who kept asking me when I was actually going to "Do It." My heartfelt thanks to you all.

Printed by Thomson - Shore, Inc. in the USA
10 9 8 7 6 5 4 3 2

Published and distributed by:

Nature Works
PO Box 469
Talent, OR 97540

For book reviews and ordering information visit **www.natureworksbooks.com** or e-mail **irene@cdsnet.net**
This book is printed on recycled paper.

Contents

Canyon Country Geology

Geology (jee-ALL-uh-jee)
Geo = "the earth"   logy = "to speak of or study"

In most places, you can't really see the earth. Oh, sure, you can scrape away plants and look at dirt, or peer into a building excavation to see what it's like underground. But the earth tends to get covered with plants and trees, and unlike the western U.S., much of the eastern U.S. is flat or has gently rolling hills. On much of the Atlantic coast, the only visible geology is where the ocean has washed away beach dunes to show layers of older beaches. Too bad for geologists!

In the canyon country of the west, it's a far different story. Weather and major *cataclysms* (KAT-uh-kliz-ums) like earthquakes, volcanic eruptions, and slowly rising mountains have made the geology extremely visible. You can't MISS it! In fact, you can see rock layers that used to be ocean bottom, or mud that dinosaurs walked on, or ancient trees turned to stone. It's all spread out before your eyes in brilliant colors on the cliffs of the redrock canyons.

Geology Words to Keep

It's hard to talk about something if you don't know its name. Here are some canyon terms:

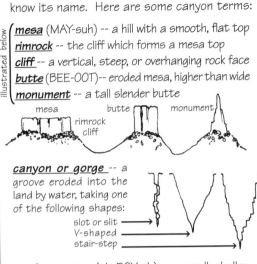

mesa (MAY-suh) -- a hill with a smooth, flat top
rimrock -- the cliff which forms a mesa top
cliff -- a vertical, steep, or overhanging rock face
butte (BEE-OOT)-- eroded mesa, higher than wide
monument -- a tall slender butte

canyon or gorge -- a groove eroded into the land by water, taking one of the following shapes:

slot or slit
V-shaped
stair-step

wash or arroyo (uh-ROY-oh) -- a small, shallow, dry canyon, wet only when it rains or snow melts; it may be only a few yards wide

gully -- a V-shaped dry "canyonette," even smaller than a wash or arroyo

joint -- a break in the bedrock between two rock surfaces
sand dune -- sand piled into a hill by wind action
fault -- a split between two rock surfaces that has moved and may move again (over the eons) up, down or sideways (it looks like a joint, but the layers don't match)
graben (GRAH-ben) -- a fallen block of earth between two faults
horst -- the high rock surfaces on both sides of a graben
laccolithic mountain -- a low mountain formed when molten rock pushed up in a blister instead of erupting as a volcano

---

incised meander (mee-AN-der) -- an S-shaped river course first formed in sediment, then worn down through rock

arch or window -- an opening eroded through rock

natural bridge --an arch in rock created or worn by a stream

volcanic plug -- the remains of lava which hardened in the neck of a volcano, and from which the outer layers have eroded away
talus -- (TAY-luss) a slope of broken rocks, fallen from a cliff
anticline -- an earth wrinkle that folds up instead of breaking
syncline -- an earth wrinkle that folds down instead of breaking
monocline -- half a syncline or anticline, with one surface high and one low (see below)

Cryptobiotic Soil

Cryptobiotic (KRIP-toh-by-AH-tic) soil (also called cryptos (KRIP-tohz) is that crunchy crust on the desert floor that turns to dust if you step on it (**don't**). In Greek, kryptos means "hidden" and biotos means "life." This crust is the soil which every plant in the desert requires for survival.

Cryptos is a combination of algae, lichens, mosses and fungi that slowly spreads through moist sand leaving behind a web of filaments. These filaments glue sand and soil together so that plants can grow there. Cryptos starting in a pothole may collect and glue together so much soil that it eventually bulges out of the pothole. In other places it forms right on the sand -- but it may take hundreds of years to make enough soil for plants to grow in. Don't step on it! It's alive -- and when crushed by footsteps or wheel tracks, it blows away leaving barren sand where nothing can grow.

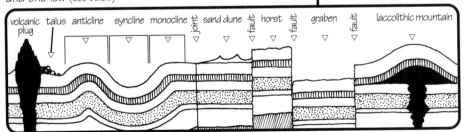

Chapter 1. Canyon Country Geology

Okay, here's the situation. The Earth is about 4.6 billion years old. The very deepest cross-section in the Colorado Plateau, the Grand Canyon, takes us down to rock layers about 2 billion years old, but the canyon itself is only about 5.5 *million* years old (one-tenth of one percent of the Earth's age). Plants have existed for only the last 20% of that time, animals only the last 10%. And humans? Don't blink -- you'd miss it!

How can the canyon be younger than the rock layers? Well, throughout the ages, the Colorado Plateau has been a lot of different things: an inland sea, an immense collection of sand dunes, a gigantic marsh, and plains partly covered by lava and ash. The meandering (mee-AND-er-ing -- snaky, slow-moving) young Colorado River, was part of the scene, but it was sometimes blocked off entirely for millions of years by earth movements. Earth continued to heave, mountains rose, valleys sank -- all in slow motion, of course, just as it does today.

When the San Andreas Fault cracked open the Gulf of California 5.5 million years ago, the plateau lifted about 3,000 feet -- *more than half a mile!* The Colorado River suddenly had a steep exit and began to cut and erode away what is now the Grand Canyon in its powerful race to the Gulf.

It cut down through layers of rock laid down for millions, then billions of years until it reached the depth at which it flows today. It's still cutting, and we can read the layers it has uncovered like the pages of a book (like the **edges** of the pages, anyway). Actually, we feel pretty lucky when a fossil washes out from between those rocky pages.

You might think that one rock is pretty much like any other. No WAY!

Each rock layer has its own makeup. No other layer has exactly the same color, hardness, composition, type of cement gluing it together, and so on.

One layer of sandstone may sculpt gently while sandstone of a different layer, harder and more brittle, may fall away in chunks. Another layer may be a totally different color or *crossbedded* (more about that later).

Some major rock types you will see in the canyon country are sandstone, limestone and shale:

<u>*sandstone*</u> *-- **petrified sand dunes or beaches,*** often with layered patterns. The Navajo Sandstone layers contain spectacular examples of fossilized sand dunes, with the sweeping lines of each dune still in place just as they were blown there by ancient winds. You can see which way the wind was blowing when the dune formed. If the wind started blowing a different direction, making a dune with more than one drift direction, we say it is crossbedded.

<u>*limestone*</u> *-- **seabed deposits,*** often containing fossils of sea life. For example, Moenkopi Limestone was deposited (accumulated or built up) in tidal mudflats, in marshes and floodplains, and along slow streams. Limestone shows ripple marks, mud cracks, pockmarks from rainstorms, sea shell fossils and tracks of land and water animals.

<u>*shale*</u> *-- **ancient mud deposits,*** often containing tracks of animals -- including dinosaurs -- and fossils of plants. The Chinle Shale, which contains volcanic ash, also contains lots of petrified wood.

This dinosaur track was found in the Kayenta Shale Formation

Much of the intense color in the canyon country comes from minerals like iron oxide -- in other words, *rust.* For instance, the reds, pinks and yellows come from iron oxide deposited by groundwater seeping between clear quartz sand grains of the original sand dunes. Greens and blues are from unoxidized iron minerals, and lavenders come from manganese. Desert varnish (see page 84) adds the finishing touches.

Red, orange, rose, lavender, green, blue, beige, ocher, burnt sienna, grey, gold, cream, and tan often lie in layers right next to each other! Whew!

That's the canyon country, rich with rocks. And it's all some people see -- the rocks. They think the landscape is dead and barren. But a closer look into a canyon will reveal hidden life that isn't visible at sixty miles per hour. Even if you can spare only a few minutes, take time to visit some part of the canyon world (see the map inside the back cover).

Redrock Canyon

Redrock -- informal name for red sandstone, found worldwide
Canyon -- from the Spanish *"cañon,"* meaning "a large gully"

The Redrock Canyon of this book is like many canyons found on the Colorado Plateau. The surrounding country is high desert, a land of plants and animals that do well in a place with hot daytime temperatures in the summer, cool nighttime temperatures year around, and in areas away from the streams, a dry place with little water available for most of the year.

The high desert is an arid habitat of piñon pine trees and juniper trees, sagebrush and cactus and much more, where thunderstorms come suddenly, drop lots of rain, and the earth dries out immediately. The soil is not rich and deep because there isn't a lot of thick vegetation to rot and turn into humus.

Here a cross-section of geology is visible from top to bottom, revealing the earth's history from the Pre-Cambrian Era, more than 570 MYA (million years ago) to the present -- right now. (See page 112.) Ancient cliff dwellings dot the canyons.

If you look hard, you may spot ancient Indian cliff dwellings and granaries that aren't on any maps -- even while traveling on the highways (see page 54).

Who Needs Scientific Names?

A single kind of plant or animal may have a lot of different names. For instance, the animal scientists know as **Felis concolor** is also called the cougar, panther, mountain lion or puma. In Spanish-speaking countries, it is called *león*. But its scientific or <u>species</u> (SPEE-sheez) name always stays the same -- *Felis concolor* -- everywhere.

Species names are always in *italics*. The first name is the <u>genus</u> (JEE-nuss), and its first letter is capitalized. The <u>specific</u> (spuh-SIF-ik) name follows and is *usually* not capitalized. They're often Latin or Greek words.

Scientists work hard to give every living thing a scientific name.

For example, many quite different plants are called "ironwood." But each living thing has only <u>one</u> scientific name. So if you know the species name, then you know exactly which "ironwood" it is.

Please Pass the Salt

Salt and *alkali* (AL-kuh-lye) are some of the natural minerals found in soil. Moisture evaporating from the soil leaves minerals behind on the surface. In wetter climates, these minerals wash into streams and away into the ocean -- that's why the ocean is salty. But in hot deserts, rain water evaporates instead of flowing away, leaving the minerals on the desert's surface. The soil becomes so mineralized that only a few plants can live there. The four-winged saltbush deals with extra salt by storing it in its leaves (along with oxalic acid which stings a nibbler's mouth).

Plants have adapted in different ways to deal with hot, dry, mineral conditions. Some "shut down" when it gets too hot. But the silvery surface of buffaloberry leaves reflects heat instead of absorbing it as other plants do. Cactus spines are actually sharp "leaves," so hard and tough that moisture can't escape from them. Some plants produce white fuzz to shield themselves from the hot sun. Shrubs like the sagebrush produce extra bark layers to insulate their stems from heat. Junipers may have several inches of shredded bark protecting their trunks. Columbine and ferns grow on the cooler shady sides of canyons, and needn't be so tough.

barrel cactus

Because there are few plants to anchor the desert soil with their roots, or mulch it with leaves and twigs, wind and rain can blow and wash the unprotected soil away, making gullies and canyons that expose their rocky history. Geologists love canyons!

Carving a Canyon

Flash floods play an important part in the formation of canyons. The redrock canyon in this book began as a simple crack in the rock at the top of the mesa. A small trickle of water dripped down through the crack and wore away grains of sand until the crack became a *crevice* (KREH-viss -- a narrow opening). A pebble falling into the crevice plugged it partway down, creating a small waterfall during storms. The waterfall eroded the sides of the crevice until eons later it extended to the base of the mesa. Now it was a small canyon.

Lichens (LIE-kenz), plant groups of fungi and algae combinations, grew on the rocks and produced acids which broke down the cement holding the sand grains together. Sand, blown by wind, ground away the sides of the canyon.

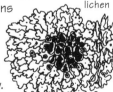

lichen

Rainstorms carved and deepened it over millions of years, exposing different layers of stone, some fragile and quickly wearing away. Some layers of stone absorbed water more quickly than others, causing them to swell and break away. Further erosion (ee-ROH-zshun) exposed a small spring of water which seeped down the side of the canyon.

Earthquakes caused parts of the canyon to collapse. Water in cracks, swelling as it froze into ice, forced blocks of stone to break off, crushing the rocks below as they fell. Flash floods scoured the canyon and carved out potholes until it appeared as it does today -- and it's still changing.

Compared to geological time, when things happen over <u>eons</u>, individual humans live for only an instant. Wouldn't you love to hover overhead and run the whole show by at high speed so you could see it in action?

Chapter 2. Living In The Canyon

You may never find the redrock canyon featured in this book. But it's real enough. All of its ecosystems exist and the wild animals that live there have the experiences you can read about in this book. But much of what happens is hidden from sight and you might not realize it from just a casual look....

In most places wild animals are wary of people and hard to find or approach close enough to watch. Often when you see a wild animal it is not doing its usual stuff -- it is busy watching YOU. And in the desert and the canyon country where you can see for miles and nothing is moving, it's easy to get the idea that hardly anything lives there anyway. WRONG!

There are gazillions of critters out there, keeping quiet, keeping cool, watching each other and watching you. Most of them will stay out of sight as long as you stick around -- unless you find a place where you can hunker down and stay quiet for awhile to watch. If you're talking, yelling, walking noisily, tossing rocks or driving through in a car, you might not see things. It's up to you.

So what do wild creatures do when you're not around? What do they do after dark? What do they eat; what eats them? Which of their neighbors do they fight, and why? Which do they get along with just fine? What strange and amazing things happen in their lives that you couldn't even guess, even if you tried?

If you could fly like a bird or bat, creep into tiny cracks like a lizard, climb near-vertical cliff faces like a ringtail, enter small tunnels like a mouse, and swim underwater like a minnow -- just *imagine* what you could discover! And if you were invisible? Yeah!

Many scientists, naturalists and ordinary people who love wildlife and the outdoors have spent their lives watching animals, taking notes and photographing them. With cameras, pens and notebooks, they've observed things and recorded them. In this book, many of those observations have been put together like pieces of a jigsaw puzzle to make a picture of canyon life that is very close to reality. There are many canyons very much like this that you can explore, if you want to.

> **Read the right-hand pages like a story.**
> **Read the left-hand pages for more details.**

Learn what happens in the canyons and why, and how it all connects into one interwoven web of amazing life --

* from one animal to another,
* from one place to another, and even
* from one time to another.

And, just as in real life, one thing leads to another, from one chapter to the next.

> Be sure to check the map of the canyon inside the cover to see where things in the story are happening. Starting on page 106 are some fun things you might enjoy doing.

And now, welcome to Redrock Canyon.............
a place where the ruins of ancient Indian dwellings lie undisturbed and animals go about their business without any people around.

It's the end of a warm spring day. The cliffs glow like jack-o-lanterns in the orange light of sunset. The sharp, pungent scent of sagebrush drifts on the breeze. A few crickets have started to chirp, and the "cooo_o" of mourning doves drifts through the canyon shadows.

Suddenly a wild, wavering cry splits the air. The quiet evening sounds pause, and for a moment all is still. Then again...

"Wup-wup-wah-eeeeeeerrrrrrrrrrrr r r...."

Coyote (KY-oht or ky-OH-tee)

Canis latrans (KAY-niss LAY-trenz)
Canis = "dog"   *latrans* = "barker"

Coyotes are found from the Canadian tundra to Costa Rica in Central America, from forests to deserts and from valleys to mountains -- and they love the desert canyons.

Families hunt together until the young are grown. You might hear them begin a hunt with wild yipping and yodeling. It is one of the most marvelous sounds of the wild canyons.

Coyotes are important *predators* (PREH-duh-terz -- animals that kill and eat other animals). If coyotes didn't eat a lot of rabbits and small rodents, there would soon be so many of these little *herbivores* (UR-buh-vorz -- plant eaters) that they would eat all the green plants -- and then they would all starve. So, in a way, the coyote (and the cougar, bobcat, owl and other predators) take care of *all kinds* of wildlife by keeping the right balance between herbivores and their plant food.

Coyotes also eat juniper berries, cactus fruits and other vegetation, and dead animals they find lying around.

"Coyote" Is A Weird Word...

The coyote plays an important part in Native American religious ceremonies and legends. "Coyote" is an Aztec (Indians of Central America) word. Their word coyotl (ko-YO-tl) has a sound called a "lateral L."

your "smile"

your tongue

To sound like an Aztec, say "ko - yo," then put the tip of your tongue on the roof of your mouth just behind your front teeth, smile, and whisper "tull" (that's the *lateral L*) without moving your tongue.

The air will exit the sides of your smile and hey! you'll sound just like an Aztec. Well, maybe!

A Dentist's Dream
Coyotes can REALLY open wid

|— 7" —|

It's a Puppy, but...

coyote pup
5 weeks old

Although a young coyote puppy may look quite a bit like a German Shepherd pup, by the time it is a year old you probably wouldn't mistake this slim "songdog" for a domestic dog.

Eastern coyotes look a bit more "doggy" than western coyotes.

Nothing Lives Here!

It's quiet in the canyon. A piñon jay sits on its nest, a gray fox prowls along a trail hunting mice. A bobcat on a ledge watches the trail below. Suddenly --

"HEY, WAIT FOR ME! I bet you can't throw a rock THIS far!" Crash, thunk, thunk, rattle! *"Let's make an echo. HELLO-O-O! ANYBODY HOME? Sure is dead around here! Race you back to camp!"*

thump, thump, thump, thump, thump, thump, thump, thump, thump, thump, thump, thump, thump

"Hey, Dad, you were wrong! There's no wildlife out there!"

(oh, really....?)

Scat!
When talking about wildlife signs, "scat" doesn't mean "Get outta here!" It means animal droppings, or "poop." Scat tells you what kind of wildlife lives in the area.

Coyotes like to leave scat at important places in their territory -- on a rock, at the base of a tree, on the top of a hill. This is a wilderness "newspaper" that tells other animals (and you) about the coyote. By looking at scat and where it is placed, you can often learn who was there, how long ago, what they ate, and their approximate size.

Handling scat with bare hands isn't a good idea, but it is easy to look at it on the ground. Use a magnifying glass for small scats. Pry larger scats apart with a stick. In a coyote scat you'll find things like fur, bones, seeds, mouse skulls, rabbit teeth, feathers, and insect parts -- things it ate that were too tough for its digestive juices to dissolve.

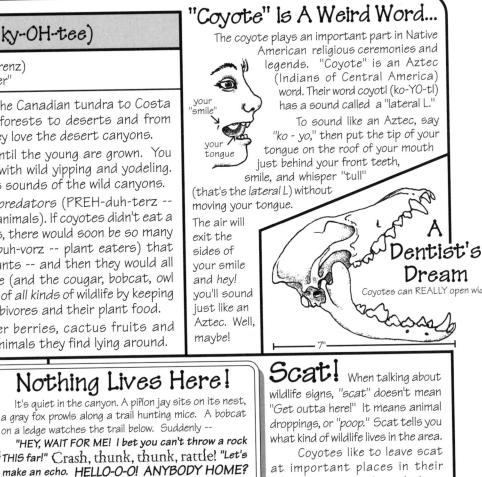

coyote scat
about 1/3
natural size

coyote track & scat

left hind foot

2½"

left front foot

· about 16" ·

walking along →

Chapter 3. The Coyote

From a point of red sandstone on the canyon lip, the coyote looked down into the canyon with sharp eyes. Blue shadows were creeping up the sandstone arch in the orange canyon wall as the sun sank behind him. A cool breeze ruffled the long hairs on his belly and the fur of the cottontail rabbit he had just caught for his family's dinner. To the east the silver moon floated up over the rimrock. A tall sandstone monument, carved by wind and rain for a million years, pointed at the sky like a finger.

The coyote shivered in the cool air and his nose went up as his wild cry filled the canyon air.

"Wup-wup-wah-eeeeeer. Wup-wup-wah-eeeeeeeeer." As his song floated off down the canyon he cocked his head and listened closely. There! From far down the canyon he heard his mate's answering howl "Wup-wup-wah-eeer," she sang. Then several squeaky notes joined in "weeeºoºoºoₑₑ ooeeeeeeeee weeeeeᵖ⁻weeeᵉeeₑₑoºoºoeeee!" as their young pups joined the concert.

The male coyote wagged his tail in delight, then snatched up the cottontail, trotted to the edge of the slick-rock sandstone and disappeared down the narrow trail into the canyon.

On the ledge at the mouth of the den the mother coyote watched over her family. The three pups were wildly excited -- this had been their first concert. The biggest pup leaped on the littlest pup, knocking it over in a tangle of flying fur. The third pup snapped with sharp white teeth at passing ears and tails.

Suddenly the male coyote was standing over them with the rabbit in his mouth. The puppies' play-growls turned into wild yips of excitement and muffled sneezing as they leaped onto the bundle of tickley fur. Soon their small bellies were round and full, and they sprawled contentedly on the dusty den floor. The female ate what was left of the cottontail, then she stepped over the pups to lie beside her mate on the ledge. And as the moonlight poured over the little family, they gently licked each other's faces.

Turkey Vulture

Cathartes aura (kuh-THAR-teez OR-uh)
cathartes = "cleanser"   *aura* = "gold" (or red)

The turkey vulture is one of nature's "undertakers." By cleaning up dead things, it helps prevent the spread of diseases. But its feet and bill aren't designed for opening up a fresh carcass, so it has to wait for dead meat to rot and get soft.

Adult turkey vultures return to favorite nest sites every year, and brood their 3" eggs about 40 days. They feed the hatchlings *regurgitated* (re-GUR-jih-tayt-id -- partly digested then cast back up) food, until the chicks are ready to fly at nine to eleven weeks. Most turkey vultures form big groups called "kettles" and migrate south together for the winter.

Amazingly, vultures keep their nests clean and tidy with no odor at all -- unless an intruder appears. Then they hiss or make a sound like a man snoring or water gurgling down a drain, and regurgitate a very smelly mess of rotten food, which seems to discourage most attackers.

Smell or Sight?

Turkey vultures find food by smell. This was discovered when workers looking for leaky gas pipelines saw vultures circling over leaky spots in the pipe. *Ethyl mercaptan,* added to give gas an odor, smells like something very dead. The vultures gathered on the ground looking for the delightfully rotten dinner they could smell but not see. What a disappointment!

Vultures also use their eyes to find food -- when one smells food and dives, others watching from miles away see the activity and follow to the banquet.

You'd think such a diet would make vultures sick, but their digestive juices are extra strong and destroy any bacteria from the carcass during digestion. The bare skin on the head also helps them avoid disease -- a feathered head would get pretty yukky (and unsanitary)!

A VERY Strange Bird

The tongue of the turkey vulture curls up on both sides, and the edges are serrated (SAIR-ayt-id -- sawtoothed). The vulture needs to peck up slippery things from a carcass (KAR-cuss -- dead body) and the rough tongue edges grab and help pull them into its beak.

A vulture can get very hot in its black feathers. To get cool, the vulture sucks up water using its curled-over tongue like a drinking straw.

Vultures also cool off by squirting excrement (EX-kruh-ment -- droppings) on their legs. This cools their skin four times faster than air (and also kills bacteria). Not a very pleasant habit, but definitely a useful one! By the way, that's why vulture legs look white -- they're actually *pink* when they're clean.

Where Do Downy Feathers Go?

Downy fuzz is simply the first part of a feather to sprout. The rest of the feather emerges and the fuzz wears off after awhile. Any bird that looks adult but still has fuzz is immature. Two months old, this chick has lost most of its downy fuzz.

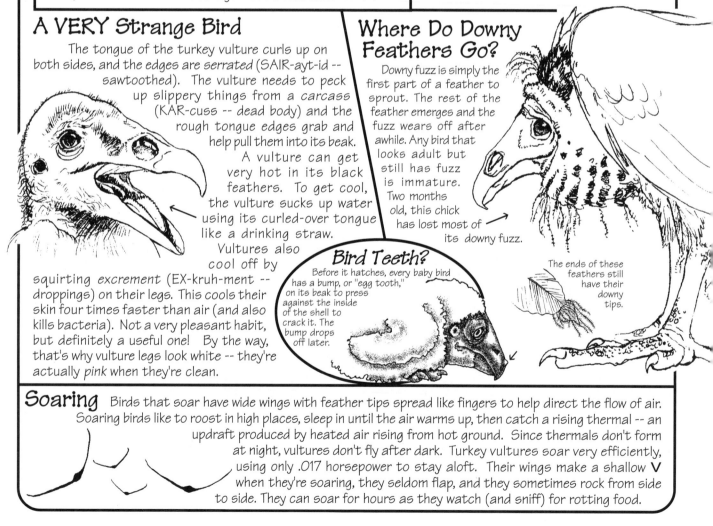

The ends of these feathers still have their downy tips.

Bird Teeth?
Before it hatches, every baby bird has a bump, or "egg tooth," on its beak to press against the inside of the shell to crack it. The bump drops off later.

Soaring
Birds that soar have wide wings with feather tips spread like fingers to help direct the flow of air. Soaring birds like to roost in high places, sleep in until the air warms up, then catch a rising thermal -- an updraft produced by heated air rising from hot ground. Since thermals don't form at night, vultures don't fly after dark. Turkey vultures soar very efficiently, using only .017 horsepower to stay aloft. Their wings make a shallow V when they're soaring, they seldom flap, and they sometimes rock from side to side. They can soar for hours as they watch (and sniff) for rotting food.

Chapter 4. The Turkey Vulture

In a cave just below the edge of the canyon across from where the coyote had howled, a dark-brown turkey vulture with a bright-red head peered out of her nesting den and fluffed her feathers. A golden eagle suddenly loomed into sight, drifting past only a few feet in front of the den, and she ducked back inside with a hiss. When the eagle finally disappeared behind some distant red cliffs, the vulture relaxed and began to groom her long, strong feathers, sliding her curved, ivory-white beak down each dark shaft.

Deeper in the cave, her newly-hatched chick, still just a tiny ball of white, downy feathers, hunched next to a brown-speckled egg. Inside the egg another tiny vulture struggled to hatch. Stepping carefully over the half-hatched egg and the nestling, the mother vulture settled down over them to keep them warm. Soon she would have two little ones to feed. Under her wing, the chick leaned against the egg and fell asleep, its shiny black head flopping limply to one side on its skinny neck. It would be several days before the chick could hold up its head for more than a few seconds.

Inside the egg, the second chick arched its neck and pressed its egg tooth against the inside of the shell to crack it, pushing with all its strength. It moved its beak a fraction of an inch and pressed again. And again. And again.

Hours later, the shell finally split into two halves and the wet chick flopped out against the mother vulture's leg. Feeling the movement, the vulture stood up and peered beneath her. She pulled out a shell and dropped it on the cave floor where it rocked back and forth. Later she would carry the shells away and drop them far from the nest. Discarding them near the nest might attract predators.

Just now the very most important thing was to keep her babies cozy. So she did.

Desert Bighorn

Ovis canadensis (OH-viss can-uh-DEN-sis)
Ovis = "sheep" *canadensis* = "belonging to Canada"

Bighorn sheep are shy and wary wanderers in the canyon country. They see people coming from far away, and find a place where they can observe but not be easily seen. Watch for them on distant rimrocks, watching you. They leap easily up steep rocky cliffs that appear to be totally unclimbable.

Bighorns prefer to eat grasses and sedges, but when these dry up, or get eaten by cattle or domestic sheep, they browse on shrubs. They need water every other day, but they often won't come to a waterhole if livestock or people are present, or if thick brush makes it hard to watch for danger.

Rams (males) band together in summer, while ewes (YOOZ -- females) and lambs form another band. In autumn, when the lambs are weaned (no longer need milk), the groups join together and are led by wise old ewes who decide where and when to move to grazing areas, waterholes or bedding spots.

Pictographs & Petroglyphs

Bighorns appear often in ancient rock art. Art may be painted (pictographs), or chipped or scratched into the stone (petroglyphs). Rock art like the bighorns above may be found in Southwest canyons.

Butting Heads

November to January is the bighorn breeding or "rutting" season. The older males have magnificent curling horns which they use in courting contests -- rising on their hind legs, racing toward each other and slamming together head-on with great crunching crashes (Rams vs. Chargers!) until one of them gives up. The winning ram gets to mate with the ewe they were both trying to impress. Both rams and ewes butt trees and shrubs to knock down fruits and berries to eat, and they crush cactus with their horns so they can get through the spines to eat the juicy insides. A big ram's horns may measure 40" around the outside of the curl.

bighorn ewe

7 yrs
6 yrs
5 yrs
4 yrs
3 yrs
2 yrs

bighorn ram

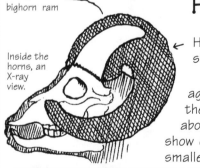

Inside the horns, an X-ray view.

Horns or Antlers -- What's the difference?

Bighorn sheep have horns, deer have antlers. They're made quite differently. Horns are constructed of hoof-like material, wrapped around a bony core and never shed. Antlers are made of bone-like material and are shed yearly. See page 68.

A bighorn's horns stop growing during the rutting season, then begin again in January. Where they stop, there is a sunken "annual ring." You can tell the age of a bighorn up to eight or ten years old by counting rings (see at left, above). After about ten years, the horns nearly stop growing and the rings don't show clearly. Young males resemble ewes because the ewes' horns stay much smaller and stop growing at four years. Ewe bighorns have a more dainty look.

bighorn track & scat

3½"

bighorn tracks aren't as rounded as deer or domestic sheep tracks.

front and rear tracks similar

about 36"

walking along → notice hind hoof steps onto front hoof print

bighorn scat about ½ natural size

Chapter 5. The Desert Bighorn Sheep

Not far from the vulture's cave, high on a ledge, several bighorn sheep ewes rested in the twilight. One ewe stood guard, watching for danger. The other ewes lay quietly chewing their cuds -- food brought up from their stomachs into their mouths to be chewed a second time.

Snuggled up to some ewes were small lambs. All day the lambs had been playing, bounding and scrambling over boulders and cliffs. Most were tired and drowsy now, but some still butted and snorted in play, not yet ready to settle down for the night.   As the shadows deepened in the canyon, the watching ewe snorted softly and all heads swung up to watch the male coyote trot down the trail across the canyon. The bighorns were safe from most four-footed predators on their high lookout, and the coyote was clear across the canyon, but wild animals must always be alert in order to survive.

Danger could come from the sky as well. A few moments later, the hunting golden eagle swooped past and the bighorns stopped chewing and watched her nervously. If the eagle had turned toward them they would have sprung to their feet, ready to defend their lambs. Bighorn sheep aren't afraid of many creatures, but they know cougars and coyotes sometimes kill sick, injured or old sheep. Ravens have been known to attack newborn lambs, and golden eagles sometimes carry away a lamb that is weak or unprotected. But this eagle passed them by, headed for the sand dunes near the foot of the canyon where kangaroo rats and rabbits could more easily be caught. The ewes relaxed again, chewing steadily and staring out over the canyon below them. One by one the lambs lay down beside their mothers, and in the light from the rising moon only the keenest eye would have noticed the silent bighorns lying on their high ledge.

Black-tailed Jackrabbit

Lepus californicus (LEP-uss cal-ih-FOR-nih-cuss)
Lepus = "hare"   *californicus* = "of California"

Black-tailed jackrabbits are the most common kind of jackrabbit in the west. Cowboys thought the long ears made them look like donkeys, so they named them jackass rabbits, which got shortened to "jackrabbits" (although they're hares, not rabbits -- see below). The giant ears are perfect for helping the hare keep cool in hot country -- blood vessels line the thin ears, and the blood loses heat when it circulates through them. The cooled blood then travels back through the hare's body and lowers its temperature.

Since a jack's bulging eyes are placed on the sides of the skull, it can see all the way around without moving. Predators have trouble catching a jack if it notices them first.

Black-tailed jacks are often seen at dawn and dusk as they travel between their brushy shelters and feeding spots, eating almost anything green, including cactus. They're the only hares having big ears with black tips, and a black tail-top.

Skull Skills -- What Is It?

If you find a skull that has *double* upper front teeth or *incisors* (in-SY-zurz) -- a small set placed directly behind the larger two front teeth -- it's a hare, rabbit or pika. Nobody knows their purpose.

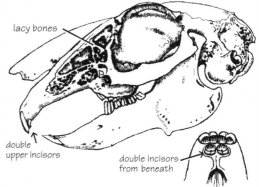

lacy bones

double upper incisors

double incisors from beneath

Also, there are lacy-looking bones on rabbit and hare skulls. A black-tailed jackrabbit's skull is about 4" long. See p. 86.

Slow Mo Joe

If you surprise a black-tailed jackrabbit far from cover, it may freeze perfectly still to avoid notice. If you move suddenly, it may make an incredibly fast getaway -- twenty-foot leaps and forty m.p.h. sprints have been recorded!

<u>BUT</u> if you freeze, too, the jack may decide to *walk* away in *v-e-r-y s-l-o-w m-o-t-i-o-n*, moving its feet in hilarious quarter-inch jerks until it is finally hidden behind a shrub. Then it will explode into activity and catapult out of sight!

Hares vs. Rabbits

Newborn jackrabbit -- it's a hare, not a rabbit.

A hare is not a rabbit. Rabbits are smaller than hares, with shorter legs and ears. But more importantly, rabbit babies are born hairless, helpless and with their eyes sealed shut. Newborn hares have silky fur, they can hop around, and their eyes are wide open and curious. It makes sense, because rabbits are born in safe burrows underground while hares are born in a nest, or "scrape," under a bush.

A bare little newborn cottontail rabbit is shown on page 86.

Jack Sign

Look for twigs that appear to have been cut with a sharp knife. Deer nibbles leave a ragged edge. See page 68.

A shallow dusty hollow may be a dust bath a jack uses to get rid of fleas. And watch for trails about 5" wide.

To understand how a hare's hind tracks end up in front of its back tracks, study these pictures →

jackrabbit track & scat

partial & complete track

5½"   front foot

hind foot tracks

· · · 9 - 12" · · ·

hopping slowly -- the hind feet always land *in front* of the front feet

jackrabbit scat natural size -- more than 500 may be produced in one day!

Chapter 6. The Black-tailed Jackrabbit

Beneath a gnarled sagebrush in the dunes at the foot of the canyon, a black-tailed jackrabbit doe lay with her four young bunnies in the shallow, fur-lined scrape (nest) she had dug. Three babies were asleep, but the fourth was exploring a clump of Indian ricegrass nearby. The shadow of the golden eagle, wings out flat in the cooling air, passed over the little family. The doe froze, eyes wide and round, ears pressed flat against her back, her heart beating fast with alarm.

Infant jackrabbits know nothing about eagles or the many other dangers they must avoid. They have to learn everything through experience -- if they get the chance. Just as the big bird flew over, the lively and curious young hare moved out from under the safety of the sagebrush.

The golden eagle instantly folded her wings and dived. Her strong claws closed around the small jackrabbit like a steel trap, killing him instantly. Without even landing, the eagle wheeled in the air and flew back to her nest with supper for her nestlings.

The mother jackrabbit didn't move or make a sound. For awhile she crouched silently. Then, very slowly, her whiskers twitched and she sat up. With one of her big hind feet she scratched at a tick which was biting her ear.   As the cool night breeze began to drift down the canyon, she tucked her three remaining babies snugly against her furry belly to keep them warm. If she missed her stolen baby, she gave no sign. And as three tiny mouths started to nurse, she sighed, closed her eyes, and went to sleep.

Golden Eagle

Aquila chrysaetos (AK-will-uh   kris-AY-ee-tohz)
Aquila = "eagle" (Latin)   *chrys* = "golden"   *aetos* = "eagle" (Greek)

People are much more familiar with our national bird, the bald eagle, than with the golden eagles which inhabit the red-rock country. The two have very different habits. While bald eagles feed mainly on fish, dying waterbirds and carrion, golden eagles eat live rodents, rabbits, snakes, and unprotected or sickly fawns. Like coyotes, they help control herbivore populations. About 70% of their food is jackrabbits and cottontails.

The "gold" in this dark-brown eagle's name refers to the gold-tipped feathers on its neck and head. It's a bit hard to see the gold from a distance. Compare the "flight profiles" below. Watch for a "flat" profile and slow, firm wingbeats.

Golden eaglets were once caught and raised by Ancestral Puebloans (Anasazi) for use in religious activities. Eagle feathers are still used in many American Indian ceremonies.

Flight Profiles

golden eagle

condor

hawk

turkey vulture

Eagle Penthouse

Eagles in the canyon country usually build their nests on cliffs overlooking the sage or grasslands where their prey lives. A nest may be used for more than a hundred years. And since the eagles add sticks and twigs during courtship each year, it may eventually be as big as a compact car and weigh more than a ton!

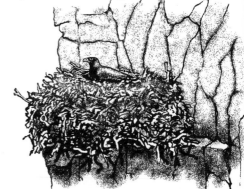

Eagle Eyeballs Rule!

An eagle can see a rabbit two miles away. WE'D be lucky to spot one ¼ mile distant! An eagle must focus both eyes on its prey to catch it, so its eyes point forward like owl eyes.

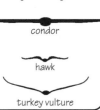

eagle vision   dove vision

predator   prey

The eyes of prey animals look to the sides and rear, to help them watch for danger from all around. Compare eagle (predator) and dove (prey) vision above.

Eagle eyes need protection against struggling prey, nestlings grabbing food, and branches during dives. Eagles blink special inner eyelids called *nictitating* (NIK-tih-tayt-ing) membranes across their eyes from front to back when needed. Other birds also have these protective transparent eyelids.

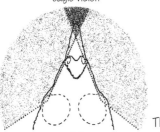

nictitating membrane

One Thing Leads to Another.....

A *food chain* is all about WHO eats WHOM or WHAT.

One plant seed, for instance, may begin the chain: The seed (see **1** below) is eaten by a jackrabbit **(2)** which is caught by an eagle **(3)** which dies for some reason and whose carcass is eaten by a vulture, insects, mouse, raven, etc. (all of which are part of other chains). Leftovers (bones, bits of meat, skin) are changed into nutrients (fertilizer) in the soil by *microorganisms* (MY-kroh-OR-gun-iz-ums) **(4)** useful to a plant **(5)**, which produces more seeds to begin the chain again. Cycles have different casts of characters each time around, and there is much about the connections we don't yet know. But if poison gets into the cycle **at any point** it can kill or weaken everything that follows. If an animal eats only a small amount of poisoned flesh, plants or seeds, it may survive. A second dose, at a later date, may kill it. Eagles are frequent poison victims. They have become rare and are now protected by Federal Law. You even need a special permit to keep an eagle feather!

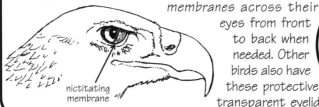

A Typical Food Chain

← start here

Chapter 7. The Golden Eagle

The young jackrabbit was a welcome addition to the golden eagle's menu. The eagle's mate had failed to return to the nest the week before, and the female, working twice as hard to feed the nestlings had spotted his body beneath a tree several miles away. Circling slowly above him, she had not seen any danger, but she was wary and left without going any closer.

Her mate had been poisoned by a raven. The raven was easy to catch -- it had fed on a dead cow which a rancher had treated with strychnine (STRIK-nine -- a poison) to kill coyotes, and it was dying. The eagle had eaten it and then died, too. Soon the poison would pass along to vultures and other carrion eaters.

But now the female eagle had two young eaglets to feed by herself and they were hungry. She paused in a ponderosa pine below her nest to strip off most of the small jackrabbit's fur and pull out the insides, then she swooped up to the huge stick-and-twig nest built on a cliff ledge, and lit on the nest edge with dinner in her beak.

The bigger chick, which had hatched several days before the other chick, shoved its way to the front and chirped loudly to be fed. The mother eagle tore off bits of the jackrabbit and poked it in the noisiest chick's mouth. Only after the large chick was full did the smaller chick get any -- not much, though, because the jackrabbit was so small. Maybe next time there would be enough for both.

As the smaller chick chirped hungrily, the mother turned and launched herself into space, off to find more food for her chicks. If she could bring home enough prey, the second chick might survive.

Only time would tell.

The Ancestral Puebloans

Ancestral Puebloans (an-SESS-trull PWEB-loh-ens)
Pueblo = Spanish for "village" or "people"   *an* = "belonging to"

The Ancestral Puebloans (also known as Anasazi) had moved away from their canyon dwellings (also called *pueblos*) by the 1300's, but no one knows why. Scientists think the weather got drier or colder and crops failed. Many villages appear to have been attacked and burned. Some cliff dwellers left their household things behind, while others moved away with all of their belongings. Present-day Hopi, Zuni and Rio Grande Pueblo tribes claim to be their descendants, and most archaeologists agree.

The Hopi people call their ancestors *Hisatsinom*. Zunis call theirs *Enote*. Some scientists call the ancient cliff dwellers *Anasazi*, while others say *Ancestral Puebloans*. It is really too bad that we don't know what *they* called themselves.

But only stone dwellings, chipped and painted rock art, potsherds (pottery chips), and abandoned household items remain where once there were thriving villages. We can only read and try to understand the signs of their passing.

"Make it do, or do without..."

Ancient peoples used natural things that many modern people probably wouldn't realize could be useful (see page 46).

*Yucca plants and juniper bark were treasured for their fibers. Yucca made strong baskets, sandals, aprons, and nets to catch small game. Fibers, still attached to the sharp leaf tip, were used for sewing. Mashed roots made soap. The fruits were eaten and the sweet stems were chewed and sucked.

*Shredded juniper bark was made into diapers and soft pads to sit or lie on, and packed into moccasins to insulate them.

*Bone scrapers prepared animal skins for clothing. Hollow bird bones became whistles. Bone needles were used for sewing.

*Feathers were made into decorations and religious offerings.

bird bone whistle

feather offerings

clay pottery cups

*Clay was formed into pots, bowls, cups, and ladles, and used in building walls.

*Pine pitch was melted onto baskets to make them waterproof.

*Flint and obsidian (kinds of stone) were chipped into arrowheads and knives.

*Large stones called *manos* (MAH-noz) and *metates* (meh-TAH-tays) were used to grind corn into flour (see below).

*Wild plant materials were used for food, baskets, dyes, and medicines.

Since everything they had was gathered or made by hand, the ancient Puebloans lived according to the old rules of "use it up, wear it out, make it do, or do without."

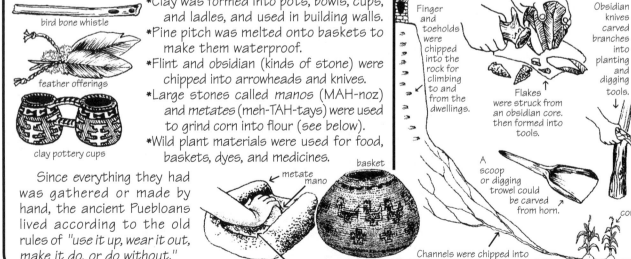

metate / mano / basket / corn

Building Code

Some Ancestral Puebloan storage shelters were built of stone. Others were wood covered with mud to keep out insects and rodents. Kivas and some houses were also built with wood. Branches were laid across the tops of the stone walls then plastered with mud to form a roof.

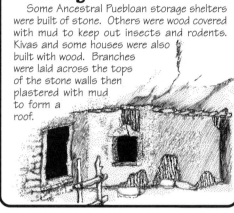

A Tree Ring Time Machine

Archaeologists (ar-kee-ALL-uh-jists) use tree growth rings to find the age of pueblo sites. Wet summers make wide rings, dry summers make narrow rings.

The archaeologists examine the rings of a *living* tree near the cliff dwelling. They find a sequence of rings (like *narrow, wide, wide, narrow, narrow, narrow*) then find the same sequence in another old tree which may go even farther back. Eventually they work their way back to trees or wood that have the same sequences as the wood the pueblo builders used in their dwelling. That gives an *exact* date for the building.

Farming Tools

The Ancestral Puebloans made tools from wood, the horns of bighorn sheep, and obsidian.

Finger and toeholds were chipped into the rock for climbing to and from the dwellings.

Obsidian knives carved branches into planting and digging tools.

Flakes were struck from an obsidian core then formed into tools.

A scoop or digging trowel could be carved from horn.

corn

Channels were chipped into cliffs to guide rainwater to the cornfields.

Chapter 8. The Ancestral Puebloans

Once, long ago, people had lived in this canyon. They had arrived at the canyon on a spring day about 800 years ago, dusty from their long walk through the warm red desert. There were black-haired men carrying rolled fiber mats, spears, bows, and arrows in quivers. They carried medicine and prayer amulets in buckskin bags. Their eyes scanned the rimrock as they walked. Strong women with babies in cradleboards on their backs carried beautiful clay pots, fur bedrolls and tightly woven baskets full of dried corn, beans and squash seeds for eating and planting. Older children toting bundles of household goods, carried tired toddlers, while young children raced ahead into the cool canyon, bundles slung over their shoulders. With the people came their animals -- dogs, turkeys, and a sacred golden eagle chick.

Scouts had found the new homesite, and had brought back descriptions of seep water dripping down the canyon walls into potholes weathered into the sandstone. They had told of well-hidden ledges where the people could build homes safe from intruders. So they had gathered up their belongings and walked.

Now, using juniper branches and yucca cord, flat stones and mud they built their houses and granaries in an airy alcove halfway up a narrow side canyon wall. They were the people we call the Ancestral Puebloans.

Like coyotes and eagles, these cliff dwellers ate jackrabbits and bighorn sheep. Like kangaroo rats and squirrels, they collected and stored grass seeds and piñon pine seeds to be eaten later. Like nesting birds and mice, they used the fibers of the juniper bark and yucca plant to make their lives more comfortable -- but while birds and mice made nests, the people sewed clothes, and made twine, baskets, mats and sandals. Like no other animals, they made stone tools, and clay pots, pitchers, mugs and ladles, and decorated them.

Just as the other canyon residents drank from the potholes below the seep, so did the people. But they alone carved grooves in the cliffs to guide rainwater from the rocks to their fields of corn, beans and squash. They stored their harvests in stone granaries high on cliff ledges or in caves. Sometimes they chipped or painted pictures on the smooth rocks.

Then, for some reason, perhaps drought or attacks by surrounding peoples, the canyon's Ancestral Puebloans disappeared. They gathered up their pots and furs and seed corn, and trekked away. Shortly after they left, a large chunk of the canyon wall fell across the mouth of the side canyon. As it fell, it knocked off other large blocks of sandstone, and when the dust cleared, the opening to the side canyon had vanished. The cliff dwellings and paintings were hidden behind a rocky plug.

No humans had entered the side canyon for nearly 10,000 full moons. Broken pots, obsidian chips, worn-out yucca-string sandals and dusty corncobs still lay where the ancient people had left them.

Northern Grasshopper Mouse

Onychomys leucogaster (oh-NIK-oh-meez LOO-ko-gas-ter)
Onycho = "clawed" *mys* = "mouse" *leuco* = "white" *gaster* = "bellied"

It's ferocious! It's carnivorous! It's a **mouse!** WHAT? Most mice eat seeds and other plant parts, but the grasshopper mouse is VERY different. Look a little closer. Even though it has only ordinary rodent teeth (see page 107, at bottom), this mouse also has long claws which help hang onto prey. It grabs a victim, pierces the back of its skull with sharp front teeth, and presto! Dinner is served! But that's not all...

Like many other carnivores, both male and female grasshopper mice scent-mark and defend territory from other mice. They may kill an intruder and eat it on the spot, or they may carry it home to feed to the kids. Unlike other male mice, a grasshopper mouse male helps feed its family and groom the babies.

For its size, the grasshopper mouse has larger adrenalin (uh-DREN-ul-in) glands than any other animal. Adrenalin causes an animal to fight instead of run away. That may be why this macho little mouse has such a "go-get-em" lifestyle!

Who's For Dinner?

A tiny but fierce grasshopper mouse attacks a kangaroo rat.

The grasshopper mouse does eat some plant parts, but about ¾ of its diet is meat: grasshoppers, adult and larval beetles, caterpillars, crickets, spiders, scorpions, lizards, carrion -- and mice and rats up to three times its size. When well-fed, it may stash a kill in an empty burrow until it gets hungry again. It seldom drinks water, getting enough moisture from its food.

Skunk Beetle

(*Eleodes sp.* = "oily like an olive")

natural size

This is one of the most common beetles seen in the desert and canyon country. It eats seeds and other plant parts. When approached, the 1½ inch-long beetle stands on its head and gives off a stink which repels most attackers. There are about 100 kinds of these beetles, also called darkling or stink beetles, and stinkbugs. Peeuw!

Dust Bath Property Lines

If you see a tiny crater in the dust about ½" deep and 2" across, it may be the dust bath of a

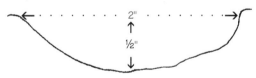

grasshopper mouse. With scent glands on its belly and under its tail, the fur of the grasshopper mouse becomes matted with musky oil unless it dust bathes frequently. The musk-scented dust baths, often placed on the edges of the mouse's huge 5-8 acre territory, also serve as "KEEP OUT!" signs to other grasshopper mice. With this mouse's reputation, that makes pretty good "scents."

Mousarrooooooooooo°°°

The grasshopper mouse often howls like a coyote. It's a very high squeal, but if the mouse were the size of a coyote, it would probably sound a lot like one. The sound carries up to 100 yards on a quiet night. Sometimes other mice join in.

But why? Maybe for the same reason coyotes howl. A grasshopper mouse howls when it leaves the burrow to hunt, before or after eating, and other times, too. Perhaps it howls to attract a mate. Or maybe just to say, "I am here. I am boss! Look out!"

mouse track & scat

natural size in dust

natural size in sand

grasshopper mouse scat, natural size

Mouse tracks are often found in soft sand or dust. A grasshopper mouse's tracks are a little rounder than other mouse tracks.

Chapter 9. The Northern Grasshopper Mouse

In the blocked side-canyon, a small mouse followed a trail at the foot of a cliff covered with petroglyphs and pictographs. Mule deer and curly-horned bighorn sheep were painted on the rock. Strange not-quite-human shapes and a lizard with a chipped-away outline mingled with gouged-out bear and rabbit tracks. Ghostly red-paint handprints patted the orange sandstone cliff.

The mouse's hunting trail followed the base of the cliff then angled out across the sand, weaving between bulgy-stemmed bottle plants and moon-white evening primroses. The mouse moved quietly along the trail in the late afternoon shadows, watching for anything that moved. A grasshopper mouse isn't satisfied with what other mice eat -- it wants meat.

An unsuspecting darkling beetle came plodding across the sand searching for something to eat. Seeing the mouse it scrambled into reverse, and as the mouse leaped, the beetle flipped up its tail to spray it with smelly liquid from glands at the tip of its abdomen. But the beetle wasn't fast enough to stop the mouse. Squinting his eyes tightly, the grass-hopper mouse shoved the stink beetle's abdomen into the soft sand where most of the spray was absorbed.

He bit off its head with a crispy crunch and ripped off the wing-covers to get at the juicy insides.

Then, leaving wing-covers, antennae, wiry legs and smelly scent glands scattered all over the sand, the grasshopper mouse sat back on his tail like a coyote and hurled a tiny, piercing howl at the rising moon.

21

Bobcat

Lynx rufus (LINKS ROO-fuss)
Lynkos = Greek for "spotted wildcat" *rufus* = "reddish"

The bobcat is found from Canada to Mexico. It adapts well to change as long as it can find a steady supply of food and places to hide. Being *nocturnal* (noc-TUR-null), the bobcat is mostly out at night, so seeing one is a real treat. If you spot a cat about 30" long, pinkish or beige with black or gray spots, a stubby 5" tail and tufted ears, it's NOT a housecat. And it won't be a lynx unless you're in the *high* mountains and extremely lucky. See the comparisons at right.

Bobcats are like housecats in some ways. They're beautiful, curious and they like to sneak up and pounce on things. They play with their food and they purr. But don't get the idea that they're just big pussycats. The bobcat is a gutsy survivor that can probably lick three dogs in a fight if it has to, can live where people have really messed up the environment, and can look out for itself just fine, thank you. *(p.s. If you see a bobcat, stay out of its way!)*

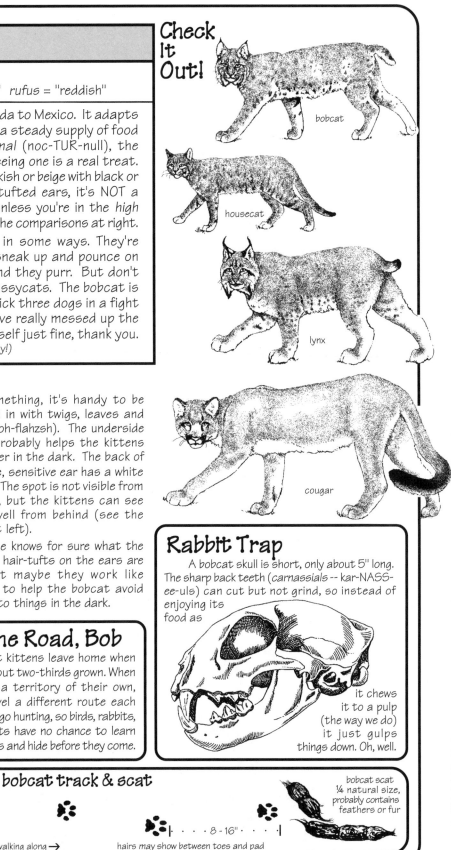

Check It Out!

bobcat

housecat

lynx

cougar

The Disappearing Trick

If you're trying to sneak up on something, it's handy to be invisible. A bobcat's spots help it blend in with twigs, leaves and shadows. That's called *camouflage* (CAM-oh-flahzsh). The underside of its black-tipped tail is white. This probably helps the kittens keep mom in sight as they try to follow her in the dark. The back of each large, sensitive ear has a white spot, too. The spot is not visible from the front, but the kittens can see it quite well from behind (see the picture at left).

No one knows for sure what the long black hair-tufts on the ears are for -- but maybe they work like antennae to help the bobcat avoid running into things in the dark.

For its size, the bobcat's feet are much larger than a housecat's, but much smaller than a lynx's (the lynx needs big feet to use as snowshoes).

Hit the Road, Bob

Bobcat kittens leave home when they're about two-thirds grown. When they find a territory of their own, they travel a different route each time they go hunting, so birds, rabbits, and rodents have no chance to learn their habits and hide before they come.

Rabbit Trap

A bobcat skull is short, only about 5" long. The sharp back teeth (carnassials -- kar-NASS-ee-uls) can cut but not grind, so instead of enjoying its food as it chews it to a pulp (the way we do) it just gulps things down. Oh, well.

bobcat track & scat

1 7/8"- 3 3/8"

1 3/4" to 2 1/8"

bobcat

1 - 1 3/8"

1 - 1 1/4"

housecat

walking along →

hairs may show between toes and pad

· · · 8 - 16" · · ·

bobcat scat ¼ natural size, probably contains feathers or fur

Chapter 10. The Bobcat

Out in the main canyon, the red cliffs deepened to purple as the sunlight faded. The full moon cast lavender shadows as it rose over the rimrock, blending the powder-black spots on the bobcat into the mosaic of ragged oak leaves and blotchy lichens on the boulders. The half-grown cat paused, almost invisible, his tufted ears switching back and forth to track faint sounds.

He listened again for a rustling noise that had come from behind a big boulder. This was new territory for the bobcat, and he had no idea what lay around the corner. Crouching flat to the ground, he waited, kneading the sand with his front paws and twitching his black-tipped tail. A raven passed high overhead on strong, slow wingbeats, blue-black feathers glinting in the sun that still shone on the tops of the mesas. The raven didn't see the bobcat camouflaged beside the rock. If it had spotted the cat, it might have circled around and landed on top of the boulder, drawing a crowd of smaller birds with its noisy croaks, and revealing the bobcat to whoever was around the boulder. But the raven flew on toward its nighttime roost, and the bobcat continued his watch.

The silence stretched out, then the sound came again -- a faint scratching rustle, like a stick dragging through sand. The bobcat crept forward, hugging the shadows. His stomach was empty and he couldn't wait any longer.

Desert Woodrat

Neotoma lepida (nee-AH-toh-muh   LEH-pid-uh)
Neo = "new"   *toma* = "cutting"   *lepida* = "pleasing"

Most people don't like rats much. When they think "rat" they think of a smelly rodent with naked ears, a scaly tail, and very dirty habits. The woodrat -- also called a packrat, because it "packs" things into its nest -- isn't the same kind of critter at all (although it may have fleas, like any other rodent). It has soft, clean fur -- even on its big ears and long tail. It is pretty, gentle, curious and very intelligent. It eats leaves and seeds, and keeps busy making home improvements.

If you camp in a woodrat's territory you may end up minus your silverware, toothbrush, or socks, depending on what appeals to the Master Builder when it stops by to visit. It may leave a stick in "trade," because it will drop whatever it was carrying to pick up the new cargo. Watch (and sniff!) for woodrat nests in cracks in cliffs, under boulders, or at the base or in the crotch of a tree. An occupied nest may have green leaves, twigs, and fresh chunks of spiny cactus around the entrance.

A Thorny Problem

If the "needles" of a cactus are its leaves, what is the "pad" (the thick, green, juicy part)?

don't look!
↓

answer: the stem

Trash or Treasure?

People who study America's ancient wildlife have discovered a time machine! They use woodrat "middens" to travel back in time. What's a midden? It's a garbage dump! Imagine what people could learn about you by going through your garbage!

Woodrats may use a nest site for thousands of years, so every scrap they collect gets glued together and preserved by their droppings and urine (this also gives woodrat nests a musky odor).

Since woodrats collect bones, plants and seeds to eat or build with, an old midden becomes a "scrap-book" of the animals and plants found around the nest area for the last several thousand years.

In Southwest woodrat middens, scientists have found plants, and bones from extinct camels, bison, mountain goats and condors from the Pleistocene era, more than 10,000 years ago. Trash or treasure?

You decide!

woodrat nest in a rocky crevice

Tooth Truths

You are likely to find woodrat skulls around woodrat nests. They are typical rodent skulls, from 1½ - 1⅞" long, with orange teeth (see page 34). The front teeth of young woodrats are spread in a **V**, top and bottom, forming a diamond-shaped notch that closes around the mother woodrat's teat. If she must flee the nest in a hurry, the young clamp on tightly and she tows them along with her to safety. Later on, their teeth straighten out. No orthodontics needed! Unfair!

A newborn woodrat -- notice the front teeth!

two weeks old

woodrat skull

Rat or Rattlesnake?

You're climbing in a canyon when you hear a sharp rattling sound. You know it was made by an animal -- was it a rattlesnake? Chances are, it's a woodrat vibrating its tail against a branch, weeds, or twigs. And in woodrat language it is saying *"Who goes there? This is my place! No trespassing."* It's all bluff, but it works -- you paid attention, right?! (Grasshoppers rattle, too!)

three weeks old

four weeks old

woodrat track & scat

hind foot   (natural size)   front foot

7½ - 8"

galloping along →

· 3½ - 4". ·

woodrat scat natural size

Chapter 11. The Desert Woodrat

Blue shadows deepened around the big boulder that hid the bobcat. On its far side, spilling out onto the sand from a narrow crack in the cliff, was a huge woodrat nest. Coyote scat, bones, and owl pellets littered the entrance, along with cactus chunks bristling with spines. The sharp spines could make any approach to the nest quite painful to predators. The sprawling nest had been inhabited by woodrat families for hundreds of years.

Five woodrats lurked inside the three entrances of the nest waiting for dark. Eyes alert, big ears swiveling, the woodrats watched and listened for danger. The shadows deepened. The hidden bobcat waited silently.

The boldest young woodrat crept out of the nest, whiskers twitching alertly. He picked his way past the cactus spines and scrambled up into a sagebrush to eat some flowers. The next young rat slipped out and climbed into a cactus which had thick, delicious pads, carefully nipping away the sharp spine tips before taking each step. The other rats scurried about harvesting flowers in nearby shrubs.

The mother woodrat was last to come out. Her belly bulged, for she would soon bear a new litter of rat pups. After eating some tender new leaves, she nipped a small cactus pad from a low-hanging prickly pear cactus and waddled with it back to the nest -- past a great horned owl pellet, part of a mule deer fawn's *vertebra* (VER-teh-bruh -- backbone), and an old woodrat jawbone. A few feet away, the boldest young rat busily dragged a rabbit leg bone through the sand toward the nest with a faint, scratching rustle. Just as the mother rat reached an entrance, the bobcat sprang from behind the boulder. A shrill rat squeak split the air and the mother woodrat was sprayed with sand and trash as she bolted safely into the entry.

Later that night, three woodrats sniffed around in the moonlight for their brother -- the one who had always gone out first and wandered farthest away from the nest. But he would never be seen again.

Further up the canyon, in the soft sand under an overhanging rock, whiskers and velvet paws twitched as the young bobcat slept off his woodrat dinner. He had found a very fine territory indeed.

Rock Wren

Salpinctes obsoletus (sal-PINK-teez ob-so-LEE-tuss)
Salpinctes = "trumpeter" *obsoletus* = "indistinct"

Visitors to desert canyons sometimes think a mocking-bird is nearby, because they hear a cheery combination of mixed calls, delivered one after the other in a lively way (like, *"chu-^{wee} chu-^{wee} chu-^{wee} chu-^{wee}, tink-^{ee} tink-^{ee} tink-^{ee} tink!"* etc.). They don't find a mockingbird, of course, for they're hearing a rock wren. The rock wren's specific name, *obsoletus* (indistinct or hard to see) suits this bird well. It could be really hard to spot, with its small size (about as big as a sparrow) and greyish feathers. But its bright song, and the way it bobs on top of rocks and flicks its tail, draw attention to it. During nesting season, though, it doesn't sing near its nest. It is very quiet and sneaky while bringing insects to its chicks, hoping nobody will notice.

While the canyon wren prefers brushy or wooded canyon areas, the rock wren can be seen in the more open drier parts. Away from the nest, the rock wren is trustful, and may let you come within a few feet of it if you move quietly.

How to Build a Rock Wren Nest

Did you ever wish you could be a bird? Maybe you should try the life of a rock wren -- and, oh yeah, it's time to build a nest.

(This will be HARD work. Since you're much bigger than a wren, most of the nest materials should be 8 - 12" long -- and remember, you must pick up and carry everything in your mouth! Your mate will help you.)

1. Collect about 1,500 rocks, seedpods, sticks, bones, and snail shells. About a third of them should be 8 - 12" rocks!

2. Pave the burrow going back to the nest area with rocks. Make a nice flat terrace or patio out in front. Build a wall across the door opening so you can just barely squeeze in.

3. It's time to build the nest. Find bits of nesting material and bring them back with you (one or two at a time, and in your mouth, remember). To keep things in scale, use big weeds and slender, springy sticks like willows. Bring feathers and bighorn wool, too.

4. To hollow out the nest cup, squat in the pile of sticks and turn around and around. Of course, the nest is at the end of your 12-15' long burrow (that's two or three times your length) so it's really *dark*. Now you can lay your eggs.....

5. Aren't you glad you're not really a rock wren?

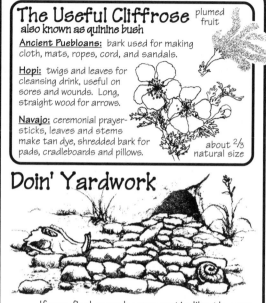
Doin' Yardwork

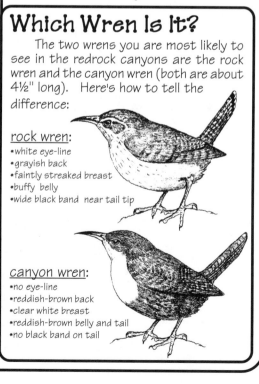

If you find a rock wren patio like the one above, look for a spot about fifty feet away to sit and watch the adults bring food for the chicks every few minutes (if they have chicks in the nest). The terrace is made of small stones, ½" to 1" in diameter, small sticks, bones and other hard items. Rocks are stacked like a brick wall at the entrance.

Don't hang around too long, or disturb the patio or opening. The parents won't bring food for the chicks if you're too close!

Which Wren Is It?

The two wrens you are most likely to see in the redrock canyons are the rock wren and the canyon wren (both are about 4½" long). Here's how to tell the difference:

rock wren:
• white eye-line
• grayish back
• faintly streaked breast
• buffy belly
• wide black band near tail tip

canyon wren:
• no eye-line
• reddish-brown back
• clear white breast
• reddish-brown belly and tail
• no black band on tail

Chapter 12. The Rock Wren

A tuft of the missing woodrat's fur showed up in a rock wren's nest the next day. The female wren spotted the gray fluff caught in a cliffrose bush covered with small, creamy, roselike flowers. She watched the fur for a moment to make sure it wasn't dangerous, then she plucked it off the thorns and carried it away to her home in a pile of boulders on a ledge across the canyon from the woodrat den.

Her nest was hidden deep in an old mouse burrow, and the entrance was paved with eighty or ninety small, flat stones making a sort of patio. A wall of pebbles partly blocked the burrow opening. She squeezed inside and down the twelve-inch-long tunnel to the nest she and her mate were building. As she poked the tuft of fur into the grassy nest cup, her mate sang from a black-brush (page 86) nearby. The songs sounded happy and cheery -- "Ka-reeee, ka-reeee, ka-reeee, wheet-eer, wheet-eer, wheet-eer, chee-poo, chee-poo, chee-poo, chee-poo" -- but they were sung to warn away any other wren who might want to build nearby. When the woodrat fur was tucked in, the female wren popped back out onto the patio and flew off down the canyon in a series of jerky flights, tail flipping up and down as wrens' tails do.

The canyon floor was laced with a silvery trickle of running water from last night's rain. She stopped for a drink, then flew to the cottonwood tree at the foot of the canyon. Under that tree she knew she would find downy white cottonwood seedpod fluff. She flew a bit faster -- her nest wasn't ready yet and she could feel that it was almost time to lay her eggs.

White-tailed Antelope Squirrel

Ammospermophilus leucurus (AM-oh-spur-MAH-ful-us LEW-kur-us)
Ammospermophilus = "sand and seed lover" *leucurus* = "white-tail"

FLIK! "Did you see that?" "No." *ZIP!* "Wait, I saw it!" *FLIK-ZIP!* "Saw what?" *ZIP!* "There! Between those shrubs." *ZIP-FLIK!* "What IS it?!?!" Keep watching and you'll probably see a little ground squirrel with its white tail curled up over its back, racing from seed to greens to an occasional insect at high speed. The white-tailed antelope squirrel may eat what it finds immediately, or it may stop to cram its treasures into its cheek pouches with its front paws. Then it dashes for its burrow to cool off for awhile. It often eats with its cheeks full (don't try this around your parents unless you're looking for trouble).

Most desert animals hide to keep cool in the daytime. But this squirrel can take more heat than most other animals, so it can harvest its food while squirrel-eating coyotes and rattlesnakes are asleep in the shade. Very alert, it flicks its tail up and down and gives a loud, chirpy trill when disturbed. Look for its tracks in sand (for fun, try "reading" the tracks on page 29).

The Feast
An amazing variety of seeds, fruits, flowers and insects are snatched up by the antelope squirrel, stuffed into the roomy cheek pouches, and carried home to eat or store for later. Here are some:

scalloped phacelia → *Phacelia integrifolia*

green brittlebush → *Encelia frutescens*

prickly pear cactus → *Opuntia*

four-wing saltbush → *Atriplex canescens*

Fremont barberry → *Mahonia fremontii*

Utah juniper → *Juniperus osteosperma*

crickets

flies

grasshoppers

Jerusalem crickets

What Could It Be?
There are three types of <u>striped</u> squirrels in the canyon country: chipmunks (several different species), white-tailed antelope squirrels, and golden-mantled squirrels. Here's how to tell them apart:

various chipmunks

white-tailed antelope squirrel

golden-mantled squirrel

Body 3 2/3 - 6," variable color, stripes on body <u>and face</u>.

Body 5½ - 6½," no face stripes, pinkish gray, tail <u>white</u> beneath -- grey on top.

Body 6 to 8," no face stripes, golden head & shoulders, <u>dark</u> tail.

Home Sweet Home
Antelope squirrels have two kinds of burrow: An escape (or cooling) burrow is shallow with no nest. A nesting burrow has a soft nest in a large 6-10" hollow and several side rooms for storing food or for use as toilets. Both types of burrow have several exits.

← escape exits →

escape burrow cross-section

storage rooms

toilet

storage room

rock

Fur, soft plant fibers and feathers are used in nest.

nesting burrow cross-section

Beating the Heat

The antelope ground squirrel has ways to beat the heat. Its white tail, carried over its back, reflects heat and shades its body. In sunshine, gathering food, it remains comfortable until its body temperature rises to a sizzling 110.°

On an ordinary hot day, it cools off by diving deep into its burrow and pressing its body to the cool soil. When the ground temperature rises to 120° - 140° it will drool large amounts of saliva and rub it over face and head with its forepaws to let evaporation lower its temperature.

white-tailed antelope squirrel track & scat

hind foot

1 3/8"

front foot

3 - 3¼"

6 - 15"

bounding along →

scat natural size

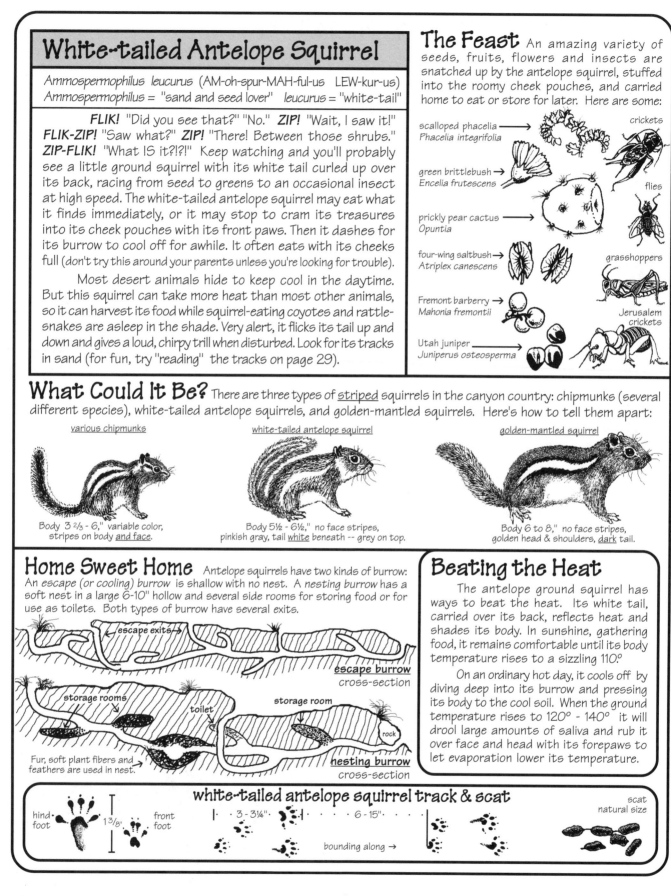

Chapter 13. The White-tailed Antelope Squirrel

Scurrying around in the shrubby sand dunes near the cottonwood, a small, white-tailed antelope squirrel searched for seeds with quick, jerky movements. His short white tail flicked up and down as he ran, like the tail of a pronghorn antelope. He was looking for seeds to tuck into his cheek pouches and carry back to his burrow beneath a four-winged salt-bush at the foot of a steep bank nearby. Already his cheeks were bulging with several kinds of grass seeds he had collected to store in his underground chambers. But meanwhile, his stomach was grumbling with hunger. He scuttled up the springy branches of a leafy shrub, braced himself in the swaying twigs, and chewed off the tender green tips. The noonday air shimmered with heat and the shrill buzz of cicadas in the desert sunshine.

For awhile, the antelope squirrel was able to keep cool under the shade of his white tail, held up over his back. But finally, even that wasn't enough. Hot and panting, he leaped down from the shrub. He snatched up a four-winged saltbush seedcase, tamping it into an already-crammed cheek pouch with his forepaws. Popping into his burrow in a puff of dust, the antelope squirrel scurried to the storage chamber, where he combed the seeds out of his pouches and shoved them against a heap of seeds that already nearly filled the room. Then he trotted along his burrow, feeling his way in the dark with sensitive whiskers until he got to the first empty side tunnel. Flopping down on his belly and closing his eyes, the little squirrel sighed with pleasure as the moist earth began to cool his body.

Badger

Taxidea taxus (tax-ID-ee-uh TAX-us)
Tax = "to arrange" *idea* = "a thing's appearance" *taxus* = "badger"

The badger, weighing in at 15 to 25 pounds, is the "tank" of the animal world. It is low and squatty, well-armed, and heavily protected -- you wouldn't want to meet a badger in a dark tunnel. Most of the critters who do end up as lunch.

Digging with its sturdy 2" front claws, and pushing the dirt backward with its flat, shovel-shaped back claws, the badger throws up a plume of dirt behind it and disappears into the ground in seconds. A mound of dirt, three to eight feet across and up to two feet high with an entrance the size and shape of a squashed basketball, is probably a "badger dig." It could be the badger's den, descending six to ten feet, or it may be where it dug up a snack. Badgers eat mostly rodents -- ground squirrels, chipmunks, gophers, prairie dogs, kangaroo rats and mice.

Badgers are members of the carnivorous weasel family, *Mustelidæ* (mus-TELL-ih-dee), and are related to skunks, black-footed ferrets, otters, wolverines and, of course, weasels.

Geaster

Watch for geasters (JEE-ass-ters, *ge* = earth, *aster* = star) lying on the sand like potbellied starfish. A geaster is a puffball, a sort of mushroom, whose cover has peeled away like rays of a star from its round spore sac. When the spores ripen, they puff out through a hole in the top of the ball and drift away.

— actual size

Myth or Truth?

For years Westerners have told about coyotes and badgers hunting together, with the badger doing the digging, and sharing with the coyote whatever it digs up. Navajos have legends about Badger and Coyote cooperating. Cowboys and ranchers told similar stories, but they seemed to be just more of those "Aw, c'mon!" sort of tall tales. But a badger biologist doing a study in Wyoming recently discovered that

A Hardheaded Hunter

badger skull

|← 5" →|

The badger has an extremely tough skull. It *needs* one. A badger uses its head as a shovel to push dirt aside, and sometimes as a wedge to force small tunnels open. A badger's heavy-duty skull weighs almost *twice* as much (about 4 ounces) as a raccoon skull the same size (about 2 ½ ounces).

coyotes really DO hang out with badgers. With longer legs and keener eyes, a coyote will actually locate a distant rodent (like a ground squirrel or prairie dog) and lead the badger to it. The badger starts digging and follows the rodent underground -- sometimes 9 - 10 feet down. With a coyote waiting outside to grab it, the rodent is afraid to come out -- so the badger has a better chance of catching it underground. But if a desperate rodent DOES pop out, it's history. In fact, coyotes hunting with badgers catch about a third more rodents than coyotes hunting alone. And that's no myth.

badger   black-footed ferret   striped skunk

Masked Stinkers

Many members of the weasel family are boldly marked (more about this on page 50). Here three, all of which have well-developed scent glands. *Particularly the "fragrant" skunk.*

badger track & scat

left hind foot   2¼"   left front foot

← left feet - walking - right feet →
notice toes point inward

|· · · · 6 - 12" · · · ·|

badger scat
2/5 natural size

Chapter 14. The Badger

Waddling through the sand dunes on his short, strong legs, the low-slung badger swung his flat head into the hot breeze. The scent of a porcupine drifted to him from the cottonwood tree near the beaver dam. He shook his head with irritation and snorted the porcupine smell out of his nose. He wanted nothing to do with porcupines -- a recent meeting with one had left quills in his foreleg. It had taken days for them to work their way out through the skin. He paused for a moment at the memory, licking the sore spot on his wrist, then turned his attention to the breeze again.

He zeroed in on a steamy scent drifting from a burrow entrance beneath a four-winged saltbush. Pushing his nose into the hole, he took a deep sniff to make sure the burrow was occupied. It definitely was.

The badger backed up and turned his head in a slow arc, studying the surrounding area until he spotted a similar hole. After inhaling sharply at the second hole, he nosed some loose soil into it, tamping it in firmly with his nose, and went to search for another. When the badger had blocked all the entrances he could find, he went back to the first hole where the scent had been strongest. His long claws and powerful shoulder muscles went into action, filling the air with a geyser of sand and dust, one dried geaster and a drift of saltbush seedpods.

Within seconds, the badger had dug himself nearly out of sight. Inside the mound, the napping white-tailed antelope squirrel awoke in panic to find himself cut off from his escape exits by the hungry badger. But he wasn't frightened for long -- the end came quickly.

After the squirrel dinner, the badger lay on his side in the tight tunnel and scraped away several inches of sand, enlarging the narrow shaft into a more comfortable sleeping cavity. His stomach gurgled pleasantly as he settled down to doze. This would be a perfect place to sleep off his meal.

Porcupine (Latin for "thorny pig")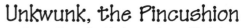

Erethizon dorsatum (air-uh-THY-zun dor-SAY-tum)
Erethiz = "to make angry or excite" *dorsatum* = "the back"

What mammal perches in trees, poops wood-pellet scats, has poor vision and hearing, and looks like it might be the offspring of a pincushion and a blackberry bush? The *porcupine*? *Right!* (Wow, did you read the chapter title, or *what*?)

With its large size (15 - 25 lbs) and prickly quills, you aren't likely to mistake the porcupine for any other animal. It's fearless -- like the skunk, the porcupine figures it is safer to stand and fight than to run. And it's usually right.

The slow, nearsighted porcupine may seem stupid, but its excellent memory enables it to remember where it found the best food last year. Whiskers and quills provide a keen sense of touch, and the porcupine smells food carefully before making a selection. A porcupine hears about as well as humans do.

Its winter diet is bark and twigs. Other times, it eats such things as acorns, plant leaves, seedheads and flowers.

Genius it *isn't*, but the porcupine has all the brains it needs!

Reading Signs
Porcupines leave a *lot* of signs around. A good detective may discover quite a few.

Listen for:

"Unh, unh, unh, unh, unh, unh, unh, unh, unh, unh, unh, unh, unh, unh, unh, unh, unh, unh!"

Watch for:

A BIG DARK LUMP IN A TREE (it could be a porcupine)

TREES with patches of bark chewed off

DENS with scat piled outside entrance

TWIGS under trees, with buds and bark layer chewed off

ROAD SIGNS chewed edges of posts

QUILLS lying around

SCAT scattered under trees

TRACKS (see below)

Unkwunk, the Pincushion

Some Canadian Indian tribes called this peaceable creature *Unkwunk*, perhaps because of its "Unh! unh!" cry when mating. It also talks to itself with an amazing assortment of grunts, squeals, and moans.

When threatened, the porcupine tucks in its nose, erects all its body quills, and gets ready to swing its heavily quilled tail. People used to think that porcupines actually *threw* quills, but they don't. Sometimes quills loosen and fly off, and they're so sharp that if they hit something they stick.

Each quill has *retrorse* (REE-trorss -- backward-pointing) barbs that pull it into the flesh with every movement of the victim, until it entirely disappears under the skin. The barbs can pull the quill forward an inch per day, and if it happens to puncture something important (like the heart) it can kill. One thing it *doesn't* do, though, is cause infection.

natural size   enlarged tip, showing barbs

Scientists discovered that the barbs actually *slow* bacterial growth. Perhaps this helps the porcupine avoid an infection when it gets scratched by its own (or a family member's) quills!

Generally, only the cougar, bobcat, and fisher (a large weasel) can kill and eat Unkwunk. Only they have learned that the porcupine has no quills on its nose or belly -- so they reach under, flip it over, and kill it!

Baby Porkies
are born with 1" quills, soft at first (lucky Mom!) but hardening within half an hour. A baby porcupine only fifteen minutes old and weighing about a pound, will instinctively bristle up and whip its tail toward danger. By the time it is two months old, it will leave its mother to begin its own solitary lifestyle.

Paws With a "Dirt Bike" Tread
The sole of a porky's foot is rough and rubbery, which helps it get a good grip when it climbs tree trunks.

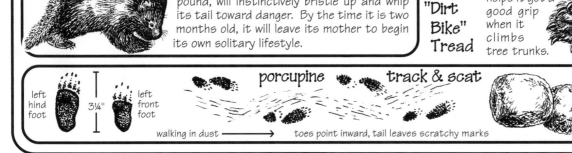

left hind foot   3¼"   left front foot

porcupine   track & scat

porcupine scat ¾ natural size

walking in dust ——→   toes point inward, tail leaves scratchy marks

Chapter 15. The Porcupine

Thirty feet up in the cottonwood tree at the edge of the stream below the beaver dam, a porcupine was dozing in the leafy shadows of her favorite sleeping-tree. The noise of the digging badger out in the sand dunes interrupted her nap, and she peered into the bright glare of sunshine, blinking drowsily. Although porcupines have poor eyesight, she could see the badger's movements in a blurry sort of way. And she knew who it was because occasional whiffs of the badger's strong, musky scent drifted up into the cottonwood tree on the hot breeze.

The porcupine listened to the enlarging of the burrow with great interest. She had been looking for

a den in which to raise her coming baby, and a badger hole makes a great porcupine nursery.

As she shifted on her high perch, a couple of quills loosened and fell from her rump. They clicked down through the twigs to land in the collection of cottonwood fluff and porcupine scat at the base of the tree. She closed her eyes and yawned, digging her long, curved claws into the bark and bracing herself against the tough bristles on the underside of her strong tail. Later, after the badger left, she just might scramble down the tree and take a look at that hole.

Beaver

Castor canadensis (KASS-tor kan-uh-DEN-sis)
Castor = "beaver" *canadensis* = "belonging to Canada"

Would you believe a beaver could turn a rocky canyon into a grassy meadow? Amazingly, it can! Here's how it does it.

When a beaver needs a home, it anchors sticks or piles rocks (if sticks are scarce) in a streambed to make a dam. The dam holds back the stream to form a pond. The pond collects fertile soil and keeps the banks moist so that trees and shrubs grow around the edges. After many years, mud fills up the pond until there is no room for water -- then the beaver goes up or down the stream and builds another dam, leaving behind a rich grassy meadow with a stream winding through where the pond once was. Without beavers, our country would look much different! Many fertile valleys would not exist.

The West was explored by white trappers collecting beaver skins. Indians were offered incredible riches to trap beavers -- they could earn an iron pot for one skin or a gun for twelve. When beaver hats went out of style in the 1850's, trapping stopped. Changing styles were all that saved the marvelous beaver!

An Island Home

Beavers have no natural defenses -- they're mild-mannered and won't fight. So they build a home, called a beaver lodge, that will keep them safe from predators.

They anchor branches in the pond mud, then add more branches until an island rises out of the water. They plaster it with mud to keep out rain. They hollow out a cavity and make a floor of mud and twigs. A hole in the floor leads down into the water and out through a tunnel. If a river is too large to dam, the beavers don't build a lodge. They live in a den they dig into the riverbank.

The Beaver's "Whole-body Toolkit"

The beaver uses its front paws like hands to hold sticks while it gnaws off the bark for food. It carries mud and sticks against its chest to build or mend its dam.

A beaver's rear paws are webbed, for swimming, and have broad, flat nails. A gland beneath its tail provides waterproof grooming oil, and a special grooming claw on the hind foot helps it spread the oil through its coat to repel water.

A beaver's teeth are enameled with iron salts which harden them and make them bright orange -- they can cut through a 4" willow tree in three minutes. Since its teeth *never* stop growing, the beaver must keep chewing to wear them down.

Underwater, two flaps of skin pull together behind the front teeth so the beaver can chew without getting a mouthful of water. Ear and nose flaps close underwater, too.

And the flat, scaly tail (see page 35) is a swimming rudder, a sitting cushion, and makes warning signals. It hits the water with a "SMACK" if danger appears.

skull

front foot

hind foot

grooming claw

flaps

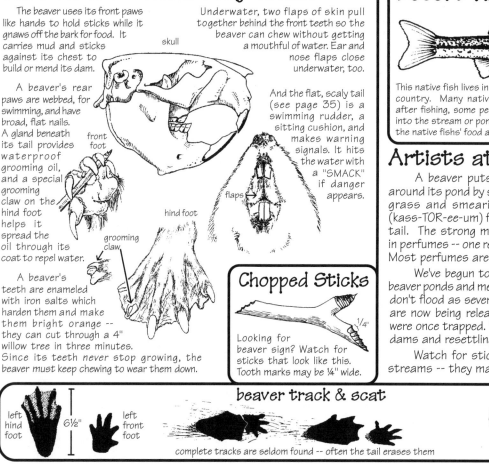

Chopped Sticks

Looking for beaver sign? Watch for sticks that look like this. Tooth marks may be ¼" wide.

1/4"

Desert Native

Speckled Dace
Rhinichthys osculus
length -- up to 4"

This native fish lives in creeks and ponds in the canyon country. Many native fish are endangered because after fishing, some people dump their unused live bait into the stream or pond. These non-native bait fish eat the native fishs' food and babies, and crowd them out.

Artists at Work

A beaver puts property line "signposts" around its pond by scraping up piles of mud and grass and smearing them with *castoreum* (kass-TOR-ee-um) from a scent gland under its tail. The strong musky scent was once used in perfumes -- one reason beavers were trapped. Most perfumes are now synthetic.

We've begun to see that ecosystems with beaver ponds and meadows have less erosion and don't flood as severely as other areas. Beavers are now being released into places where they were once trapped. They are once again building dams and resettling their homelands.

Watch for stick or rock dams on canyon streams -- they may be only a few feet long!

beaver track & scat

left hind foot

6½"

left front foot

complete tracks are seldom found -- often the tail erases them

beaver scat, ½ natural size (look underwater)

Chapter 16. The Beaver

Cool moist air swept off the still beaver pond near the porcupine's cottonwood tree. A pond might seem out of place in such a rocky, dry, spot -- but beavers are actually common in the streams of the redrock country and for thousands of years there had been dams on the creek that ran through the larger canyon at the foot of Redrock Canyon.

Long ago, when beavers had first arrived, there was only a shallow creek trickling through a narrow sandstone canyon past a few willows rooted into tiny pockets of sand on the banks. The beavers, migrating from a pond several miles downstream, had built a dam of rocks and willow branches that backed up enough water to make a pond nearly sixty feet wide and about five feet deep.

Over the years, flash floods had washed in soil and seeds (and sometimes washed away the dam, which the beavers would quickly rebuild). Now the pond was a lush, green oasis in the canyon. Below the dam, the cottonwood tree was a haven for wildlife, cooling the air, the soil beneath it and the stream flowing past.

The pond wouldn't last forever. The beaver family ate the bark of young cottonwoods and willow twigs growing in the fertile mud around the edges. After many years, most of the trees would be cut down for food, and the big rodents would have to leave to find a better food supply. Without the constant tending once provided by the beavers, the dam would finally erode away and the water would drain out, leaving a rich meadow which the trees and shrubs would slowly cover. Then beavers would return to start all over again. This had already happened dozens of times.

Right now, the pond was surrounded by tasty willows, and the beavers harvested twigs and branches daily. With such heavy pruning, the willows regrew in a spriggy mass, forming a dense screen along parts of the pond and stream. This made it easy for thirsty visitors to come, drink, and leave without being seen. But tracks remained in the rippled red mud -- some you might not expect to see in a desert canyon -- like the tracks of bear and cougar.

Cougar (KOO-gurr)

Felis concolor (FEE-liss KON-kull-er)
Felis = "cat" *con* = "with" *color* = "color"

The cougar is our American lion. It is most at home in secret wild places and it passes like mist through the landscape, hardly ever seen. We have to use our imaginations and small signs we can find (like tracks) to make it seem real to us.

But it's out there, all right, doing the valuable job of helping to keep the ecosystem in balance. Large predators like cougars eat ground squirrels, mice, rabbits, porcupines, deer and other animals. If they aren't there to do that, their prey multiplies until it has eaten everything green. Then, even *healthy* animals starve. We humans have unbalanced much of the natural system by removing big predators like cougars and wolves to "save" deer and other animals we like to hunt.

Cougars weed out sick, injured and very young animals. Because of this, the remaining healthy animals can thrive in their habitat. When cougars, wolves and coyotes stick around, you can be pretty sure the system is working.

Whatsiz Name?

Our big native cat has more common names than any other American mammal. Some say there are as many as 30 or 40. Here are some of the most common:

cougar = a Native American name
panther = the greek word for "leopard"
painter = Old West talk for "panther"
mountain lion = early settlers thought cougars were female African lions
catamount = "cat-of-the-mountain," an old New England name
león = (lay-OHN) the Spanish name used in Central and South America
puma = from the ancient Incan language

Stony Claws

Wouldn't you say the ancient Puebloans who chipped cougar portraits like this onto stone, respected their claws?

Spots

A cougar kitten is born with spots -- they serve as camouflage to help keep the kitten hidden for the first two months. Then the spots begin to disappear as longer, tan hairs replace the baby fur. A year-old kitten is spotless.

Why Cats Spray

Housecats have an annoying habit of "spraying" (squirting pee) on the furniture. Cougars do something similar. You could say it's a "cat thing." Since cougars live alone except for a short period when the male and female mate and when a mom is tending her kittens, they make "scrapes," piles of sticks scraped together and sprayed with *urine* (YUR-in) to mark their territory -- a whopping 25 to 100 square miles -- to warn off other cougars. When another cougar comes across a fresh scrape, it stops and turns back, to avoid a fight. Kittens leave to search for a territory that's free of fresh scrapes when they're about a year old, and mom goes solitary again.

Big Bird

Have you heard this joke? "What's yellow, weighs 150 pounds and says *'CHIRP'*?" The answer is "A 150 pound canary!" But it could also be, "A cougar!"

"CHIRP?" That's right! It also goes *"PURRRRRRR, PURRRRRRR,"* and *"MEEAAAOWW,"* like a giant housecat! Cougars don't roar or scream. If you hear a horrid scream in the wilds at night, it's probably just a young great horned owl. Cougars DO hiss and yowl like a WAY big housecat -- just amplify kitty sounds by ten.

And they chirp. They chirp to find each other in dense cover, to warn others, and to greet each other. So if you hear a big *"CHIRP"* in the wilderness, you probably shouldn't go looking for Big Bird!

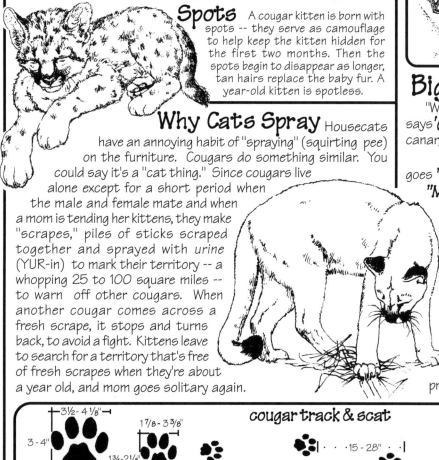

cougar track & scat

3½- 4⅛"
3 - 4"
cougar

1⅞- 3⅜"
1¾-2⅛"
bobcat

· · 15 - 28" · ·
walking along →

cougar scat ⅕ natural size. Scratch marks may show where cat covered its scat.

Chapter 17. The Cougar

A cougar crouched in a tangle of willows and watched the beavers by moonlight. The big cat had circled the pond before the beavers came out at dusk, sniffing the beaver's castoreum-scented boundary markers and twitching his long, black-tipped tail. Then he hid in the willows to wait.

But the beavers smelled the cougar, and instead of coming ashore to eat willows, they stayed out in the pond, chewing the bark off green branches they had poked into the muddy pond bottom for emergencies. The cougar twitched with frustration.

Rainfall the night before had sent a surge of water into the pond, washing away part of the beaver dam. The mother and two yearlings dragged branches from their stash and poked them into the gap. The old male dug mud from the pond floor and carried it, clutched to his chest, to tamp into the hole. Whenever the breeze brought the cougar's odor to the beavers, they dived, whacking their tails on the water with noisy splats that sent speckled dace (small spotted minnows) racing to the far end of the pond. But after awhile, the beavers would return to their mending. It took all night.

In the fiery orange dawn light, the beavers inspected their work. The trickling sounds that had triggered the mending marathon had been stopped. Tired and muddy, the beavers dived down to their lodge entrance. Safe in their den, they would groom their fur to dry and oil it, then snuggle together to sleep in a warm heap.

The cougar rose stiffly, yawned and stretched. Flicking water off his paws with each step, he waded across the stream below the dam. Wet paw prints marked his trail as he leaped from boulder to boulder, but they soon dried as the day warmed. About halfway up the canyon, just past an ancient juniper tree, the cougar flopped down grumpily on a high ledge above the trail to get some sleep. If something passed by below, he'd hear it, leap down on it and have lunch. Otherwise, it was going to be one long, hungry day.

Piñon Mouse

Peromyscus truei (pair-oh-MISS-cuss TROO-eye)
Pero = "pointed" *myscus* = "little mouse" *truei* = "for someone named True"

The piñon mouse is about the prettiest mouse you will ever see (see portrait below). In the canyon country, the soft, pinkish-grey fur of the piñon mouse blends perfectly with the red rocks and sand. But the huge, shiny black eyes and gigantic ears are what make it so charming. The eyes look like big glass beads stuck to the sides of its face. The giant ears can swivel to pinpoint the tiniest sound in any direction. Nearly an inch long ← (*this is one inch!*), those ears look as flimsy as tissue paper -- why don't they get shredded by prickly shrubs?

Piñon mice have a good attitude. They don't fight over territories and they live peacefully with each other and other *Peromyscus* mice in their neighborhoods -- probably because they can usually find plenty of food. They eat mostly seeds, like juniper and piñon nuts, and in summer they also eat insects. In turn, they are eaten by all kinds of predators like ringtails, coyotes, foxes, bobcats, hawks, owls and snakes.

Juniper Bed & Breakfast

Found alongside piñon pines and scrub oak trees in the piñon/juniper plant community, the Utah Juniper, *Juniperus osteosperma*, offers food and shelter to many canyon creatures.

Juniper fruits are called "berries," but they're really <u>cones</u>. The soft blue cone scales are fused together around a small woody seedcase that protects the single seed inside. Birds that eat juniper berries digest the blue covering while the seed in its woody envelope passes through the bird unharmed, ready to start a new tree wherever it lands. But it may not get the chance -- small rodents nip off the end of the

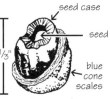

seed case
seed
1/3"
blue cone scales

juniper seed

seedcase to eat the seed inside. The entire tree is important to wildlife. The insides of dead branches rot away, but the outer wood is tough and hard to rip open. So the cavities make perfect nests, safe from hungry predators. Birds and many small mammals use the long, stringy bark in their nests.

A pile of empty seed cases below a juniper tree is a sign of piñon mice

The dense foliage hides insects and bird nests. In the hot sunshine, a juniper's life-saving shade keeps mammals, birds, reptiles, amphibians and insects from overheating. It's easy to see why the juniper is one of the most important bed-and-breakfast trees in the canyon country!

Cute, or What?

Can you find this piñon mouse on page 39? The cougar didn't.....

How Do You Say That?

Spelling can be puzzling. For instance, the word <u>piñon</u> (PIN-yohn) comes from the Spanish word for pine nut. The piñon mouse is named that because it loves to eat piñon pine nuts.

this is a piñon nut natural size →

The <u>ñ</u> is a Spanish alphabet letter called enyeh. The wiggly ~ mark over the <u>n</u> is called a tilde (TEEL-deh). The word **piñon** can also be spelled **pinyon** (it sounds the same).

The Ant Wannabe

Watch for "the ant that ain't." It's SHAPED like an ant, and scurries around like one, but the velvet ant is really a wingless wasp. It's a parasite, looking for bees or other wasps upon which to lay its eggs (when the young hatch, they eat into the insect they were laid on -- NICE characters!). A *real* ant bites with its jaws, but a velvet ant *stings* like the wasp it is -- so don't mess with it! It has a bright red, orange, golden or white velvety coat -- which warns most animals to LEAVE IT ALONE! Piñon and grasshopper mice pounce and kill before the velvet ant can sting -- few other predators dare.

velvet ant, natural size

In a Juniper Bark Nest

Chapter 18. The Piñon Mouse

A piñon mouse with gigantic papery ears had her nest in a snarl of shredded juniper bark in the crotch of the ancient juniper tree. The juniper's roots spread out over the boulders like fingers, seeking soil. Some of the old limbs branching out from the juniper crotch were hollow, and the piñon mouse's house extended deep into those cavities for safety. Living in the juniper tree was like living next to a supermarket. Only a few feet away grew a piñon pine, so there were plenty of piñon nuts and juniper seeds to eat -- that was obvious from the great heap of discarded seed shells at the base of the tree. The little mouse took advantage of the neighbors that lived in the trees, too. When nuts and seeds weren't ripe or abundant, she ate insects and spiders to fill her empty stomach. Usually, she went out only at night, but just now she had a new litter of mouse pups and she was having to work overtime to make enough milk to feed them. While searching for ripe grass seeds, she spotted a bright orange velvet ant. With a lightning-fast leap, she pounced and pressed it into the sand, biting at it with quick, nervous snaps. When it stopped moving, she ate carefully, avoiding its stinger.

A faint footstep and the rake of a twig across a furry hide -- sounds almost too quiet to hear -- brought the huge ears of the piñon mouse swiveling around. The little mouse squeezed quickly into a crack between boulders as the cougar passed by on his way into hiding. She waited for several minutes until she was sure he had gone, then raced home. Skittering up the trunk of the juniper, she kicked loose a shower of empty juniper seedcases from the crotch of the tree, and they sprayed down onto a sun-warmed boulder, right next to a sleeping collared lizard.

Collared Lizard

Crotaphytus collaris (kro-tuh-FIE-tus koh-LAIR-us)
krotaphites = "the side of the head"   *collaris* = "having a collar"

What's turquoise-blue or emerald-green with a yellow head, has two black collars, and is speckled with black and yellow dots and spots? The collared lizard! It looks like something from a sci-fi video, but you can find this native lizard in the canyon country, often perched on a rock. When you see one, you may think somebody got wild with a paintbrush.

Females aren't as colorful, but for some reason, hormone changes give them orange spots on their sides while they are carrying eggs -- the spots disappear after the eggs are laid!

The collared lizard is a big (for a lizard) fierce predator about 14" long. Its head is very large for its body. With the big head goes a big mouth, which allows it to stuff in BIG food -- such as other lizards, small snakes, grasshoppers, crickets, spiders, moths -- and its own children. **Not** a nice character.

Don't try to catch one -- they bite Big Time! They're not poisonous, but their teeth can break the skin. It hurts.

Original Lounge Lizards

Do you have trouble getting started in the morning? Feel sluggish, barely able to move? Do you love lying around in the sun? Hmmmm. Could there be a reptile in your family tree?

Lizards and snakes have a terrible time revving up on cold mornings because they're *ectothermic* (ecto = outside, thermic = temperature) or "cold-blooded." That means they need the sun to warm them up enough to move. They have just barely enough energy to creep to a spot of sunshine, and once they get there, they have to bask until they're warm enough for all their parts to work.

When they get hot, they have to run for shade to cool down because they have no "thermostat." Back and forth, all day long. Whew!

Mammals (you're one) are *endothermic* (endo = inside) -- no basking required. So what's your problem -- just need more sleep?

Visual Aids

Lizards do pushups. Up, down, up, down. Working out? No. With eyes on the *sides* of their heads, lizards can't focus forward very well with both eyes. Pushups help them judge distances better.

Try it. Close one eye, don't move, and try to guess how far away something is. Now, bob up and down like a lizard. Did moving your head help you estimate the distance a little more accurately?

More Lizards

Collared lizards lay 4 to 24 eggs in a cool moist place (under a rock, in a burrow or in sandy soil). The eggs have thin, white, papery shells. If you find such eggs, don't disturb them. They are very delicate and won't survive being handled.

natural size

Bipedalling

People, birds, and even some lizards are *bipedal* (BI-ped-ull) -- we walk or run on two feet (bi = two, ped = foot). The *basilisk* (BASS-uh-lisk) a biped lizard in Central and South America, runs on its hind feet, but only across water!

basilisk lizard

collared lizard

It streaks across the surface, its hind feet splatting the water and its front legs waving out to the sides in a comical manner. It goes so fast that before it can sink, it is already taking the next step! Local people call it the Jesus Christ Lizard because it walks on water.

The collared lizard runs bipedally too, but only on land. Still, living in the desert, who needs to walk on water?

Dinosaurs like this *velociraptor* (vuh-LOSS-uh-rap-tur), were probably the first bipeds.

A Lizard Tale

Imagine you're being chased by a 200' tall carnivore. It lunges, grabbing you by the tail (just for the moment, imagine you have a tail). You leap forward, there is a "snickkk," and your tail breaks off at a special disconnect spot. You dash off to safety, leaving the surprised predator with your tail in its mouth. (Sounds ridiculous? For you, it would be. For *lizards*, it happens all the time.)

Within a few months, your new tail will grow back where the original one was, and although it won't be as pretty as the first one, who cares -- at least you weren't lunchmeat!

collared lizard track & scat

collared lizard scat
natural size

left hind foot   (natural size)   left front foot   running on hind feet →

Chapter 19. The Collared Lizard

The bright green lizard with two black collars and lots of spots was soaking up the morning sunshine in total contentment. He had emerged about half an hour before, when a ray of early sunshine had pierced the darkness of the crack in which he had spent the night. It had brought him out to lie on the warm boulder, soaking up the warmth. But now, he began to feel actually hot. Balancing on his heels, he lifted the tip of his tail and his tender toes off the rock to allow them to cool.

Clicka-ticka-click-ticka-click-click! Click!

A sudden shower of empty juniper seedcases dislodged by the piñon mouse hit the rock all around the lizard. Instantly, the lizard was airborne in a crazy, arching leap, crash-landing six feet away in a crackle of dried leaves and juniper berries. Pedaling furiously with his hind feet, and lifting the front of his body and his tail high, he raced for safety like a miniature velociraptor dinosaur.

Normally, running for cover is a great idea, but this time the movement and the crash into the dried leaves alerted a falcon, a little American kestrel, which had been cruising past a short way down the canyon. Hovering in the air like a small kite, the cinnamon-red kestrel folded one wing and slip-slid sideways through the air to check out the noise.

With a little more experience, the kestrel might have passed the lizard by. A more mature kestrel might have already learned that collared lizards are fierce, quick, nasty customers. Their "velociraptor attitude" adds speed to their sprint and frees their front claws to grab an escaping grasshopper, lizard -- or a pursuer. And they bite *hard* when they feel threatened. But the kestrel didn't know, and her young chicks were screeching for breakfast.

She dived.

American Kestrel

Falco sparverius (FALL-ko   spar-VAIR-ee-us)
Falco = "hawk" *sparverius* = "sparrow"

Many people know this tiny (8 - 10" long) falcon as the sparrow hawk or as the killy hawk because of its *"killy, killy, killy!"* call. It is one of the most beautiful raptors, the male having powder-blue wings and the female rusty red ones. Both have "eyes in the backs of their heads" -- two eye-shaped black spots that *might* make larger predators think twice before attacking.

The kestrel is fierce and brave, ready to catch anything from grasshoppers, snakes and mice, to bats and songbirds -- and ready to chase a redtail hawk ten times its weight away from its nest vicinity in a cliff or hollow tree.

The kestrel is one of the few raptors that nest in cavities. It isn't a good nest builder -- it doesn't provide even a feather or twig to cushion the eggs and nestlings. But it is a good provider, feeding the chicks well until they leave the nest at about 30 days, fatter and heavier than their parents. The family may hunt together for the rest of the summer.

Falcon, Hawk, What's the Difference?

Falcon Family -- *Falconidae* (fall-KAHN-uh-dee),
from *falco* = "hooked claws"

* hooked upper beak with a notch
  (the notch grasps like a tooth)
* talons -- hooked claws
* wings usually long, pointed
* eyes usually very dark
* nostrils usually round with a bony knob in the hole

American kestrel

Note the "eyespot."

notch

> The falcon family includes falcons, kestrels, gyrfalcons (JER-fall-kunz)(also caracaras which have broad, rounded wings).

kestrel talon

Hawk Family -- *Accipitridae* (ak-sih-PIT-rih-dee),
from *accipiter* = "bird of prey"

* hooked beak, no notch
* talons -- hooked claws
* wings usually broad, rounded
* eyes usually yellow or orange
* nostrils oval or slitted
* fierce look caused by bony eyebrow

red-tailed hawk

> The hawk family includes hawks and eagles (and kites which have narrow, pointed wings).

Falcons and hawks are raptors (RAP-tors), which means they eat other animals. They are a very important part of the ecosystem, helping weed out unhealthy or weak mice, birds, bats, lizards, insects, etc., and keeping prey populations small so that habitats don't get overcrowded (vultures are raptors, too, and do the clean-up). All raptors are federally protected, and must not be harmed or disturbed.

Remember, it's against the law to collect their beautiful feathers.

Kestrel Kutie

Nestlings hatch from brown-speckled white eggs and are covered with white down. Male chicks are smaller and more timid than the females, but they all get along well in the nest. At first the parents tear up prey and feed the chicks bits, but at three weeks they drop the food off and let the young feed themselves. The food goes first to the chick's crop -- an internal sac which holds and pre-digests the food -- then on to the stomach. In four to five weeks the chicks are big enough to fledge (ready for flight).

crop, bulging with food

about 5 weeks old

Flight Checklist

A good small plane pilot always carefully checks and warms up the aircraft before takeoff. If the plane isn't in good condition and ready to go, it may not stay aloft.

Since the kestrel is both the pilot *and* the aircraft, it takes the time to stretch and groom carefully before launch. All muscles must be warmed up and prepared for flight.

stretching

When each feather is well-oiled, in case of rain, and meshed with the one beside it in order to hold the air, it's ready for takeoff.

Stunt Flying

If you see a small, colorful bird hovering in mid-air like a paper kite, it may be a kestrel, keen eyes alert, ready to dive at the first sign of movement below.

hovering

Sandstone Nests

Since kestrels nest in cavities, they feel right at home in the canyon country. Rain and weather often carve wonderful hollows and holes in sandstone cliffs (see "potholes," page 70). If a cavity is high on the side of a cliff, it's a perfect shelter for helpless kestrel chicks -- safe from everything but other hawks (and maybe ringtails).

Chapter 20. The American Kestrel

The kestrel was tiny -- barely 9" long with a 20" wingspan. The collared lizard was big -- about 14" long, including his tail. If the kestrel's timing had been right, she would have grasped the lizard around the body, pinned him to the ground, and killed him. But the lizard was going fast, and the kestrel's timing was a bit slow. She pinned the lizard to the ground, all right, but she had a grip on only one of his legs and his tail. The lizard whipped around fiercely and bit at the kestrel's chest, sending feathers flying.

The kestrel jerked back sharply, screaming her distress. *"Killy! killy! killy!"* echoed from cliff to cliff in the canyon. The lizard whipped back and forth in her grip, snapping wildly. A blizzard of sand, leaves and feathers filled the air.

In the wild struggle, the kestrel lost her grip on the lizard's leg -- and that cost her most of her prize. The lizard's tail, still clutched in her talons, broke off near its base. The lizard, now several inches shorter, streaked off in a crazy zig-zag to hide under a bush, while the kestrel clutched the tail and shrieked with rage.

Catching her breath and calming down, she shook her feathers back into place and took off with the spotted tail dangling from her talons. Her chicks were waiting far down the canyon inside a weathered-out hole in a sandstone cliff. With three hungry nestlings at home, part of a lizard is far better than none.

White-throated Swift

Aeronautes saxatalis (ayr-oh-NAW-teez   saks-AT-ul-us)
Aer = "air"   nautes = "sailor"   saxatalis = "a rock"

Also called the rock swift because it lives in rocky cliffs (that explains the specific name, *saxatalis*), the white-throated swift's song is a sparkling echo in the canyons. The swift is difficult to spot because it nests in cracks in the high canyon walls far off the beaten paths. But once you notice a flock, you'll watch in amazement as they whirl twittering around their home cliffs at extremely high speeds.

Like the chimney swift, which sometimes nests in suburban chimneys, the white-throated swift is *insectivorous* (in-sek-TIV-or-us), catching hundreds of insects every day -- more when it is feeding nestlings. It is a bird of the air, with tiny feet almost useless for walking, so it does everything -- eating, drinking, collecting nest materials, even mating -- while in flight.

Big feet would slow it down. Although its feet and legs are tiny, its long claws help it climb about and cling to the rock while building a nest in a crevice.

Spit 'n Feathers

Spit may not seem like such a great building material until you see what swifts can do with it! In the Far East, chefs make "bird's-nest soup" from nests that are built *entirely* of one kind of swift's gummy (yummy!) saliva. (They probably wash it before cooking.)

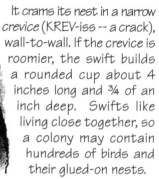

But the white-throated swift doesn't go quite that far. It just uses its gummy spit to glue feathers and other materials together and to the cliff wall.

It crams its nest in a narrow *crevice* (KREV-iss -- a crack), wall-to-wall. If the crevice is roomier, the swift builds a rounded cup about 4 inches long and ¾ of an inch deep. Swifts like living close together, so a colony may contain hundreds of birds and their glued-on nests.

Swift Or Swallow?

white-throated swift

- black on belly
- long, curved wings
- white throat
- notched tail
- black wings
- fluttery flight

violet-green swallow

- white belly
- white throat
- notched tail
- brownish wings
- smooth flight

cliff swallow

- white belly
- orange/black throat
- square tail
- brownish wings
- smooth flight

Many people mistake swifts for swallows, but you can usually tell them apart by their flight -- swallows fly smoothly, while swifts fly in an odd jerky style like bats. People used to think their wings beat alternately, left, right, left, right -- but it's just an optical illusion. Scientists have proven with strobe lights that their wings beat like all other birds' wings. Still, watch for the distinctive, batlike flutter.

The white-throated swift, violet-green swallow and cliff swallow all live in the canyon country. They're all insectivores.

They look similar, but you can use the shapes, colors and markings at left to identify them.

The peregrine falcon is supposed to be the record-breaking speedster of the bird world. But white-throated swifts have been seen out-flying peregrine falcons estimated to be traveling at 200 miles per hour! Now, THAT's "swift!"

CLAWS...

The swift's tiny claws are as sharp as a kitten's. They look like they're poking from fingerless mittens.

The Gift

If you find yourself on a cliff above swifts, try dropping a downy feather over the edge. There's a good chance a swift will snatch it right out of the air.
p.s.
Plan ahead -- take a feather!

...and JAWS !

What a sweet little bird! Such a dainty tweeter, with a tiny bill and lovely dark eyes! But then it opens its mouth and look out!

Into that gaping hole go incredible numbers of beetles, flies, termites and flying ants, bees, bugs, wasps, spiders, leafhoppers, mayflies, midges and aphids -- of all shapes and sizes.

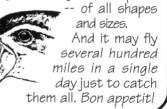

And it may fly several hundred miles in a single day just to catch them all. *Bon appetit!*

Elf Giggles

The high tinkling cry of the white-throated swift sounds much like elf laughter,

"tee tee tee tee tee tee tee tee tee tee tee tee tee tee tee teetee tee tee tee tee tee tee tee teetee tee teetee teetee teetee tee"

if you believe in that sort of thing.....

Chapter 21. The White-throated Swift

Food seemed to be on everyone's mind as dusk approached. Higher up the vertical red sand-stone cliff near the kestrel nest was a deep crevice where two rock faces met. The crevice was crammed with the nests of white-throated swifts. They had gathered grass-stems, feathers, cottonwood fluff, shredded juniper bark -- anything that could be snatched and carried away without landing -- and glued them into nest shapes with their sticky "super-glue" saliva.

All around the nest colony, the white-throated swifts flew in soaring, circling swoops, caroling streams of twitters as they dropped, then rising to circle again like swallows. A male swift, carrying a stinkbug in his beak, zoomed toward the crevice at suicidal speed.

At the last instant he folded his wings, and slipped skillfully into the crack. As his shadow darkened the nests, a chorus of hungry cries rose from all the nestlings in the colony, but he scrambled across the vertical wall headed straight for his own nest. Poking the bug into a gaping mouth, he turned and clawed his way back toward the light. At the opening, he ducked to avoid an incoming swift landing with a beakful of wasps, and launched himself back into the swirling flock.

All around him birds arrived and left, circled and dived, twittering wildly. Every day, the flock of swifts brought their nestlings thousands of insects, every-thing from mayflies caught over the pond at the foot of the canyon, to beetles plucked from tree leaves, to yucca moths fluttering near their only food source, the creamy-flowered yucca plants.

Yucca Moth

Tegeticula (several species)   (tay-guh-TICK-yew-luh)
Teget = "a covering or mat"   cula = "little"

The relationship of the yucca and the yucca moth is truly amazing. The plant and moth can't get along without each other. They depend on each other so much that each species of yucca has its own species of moth to pollinate it.

The moth is creamy-white, the color of yucca blossoms, which helps hide it from predators. The male and female mate at the flower, then the female gets busy. She gathers pollen from the stamens, pressing it into a ball with her mouth tentacles (as an adult moth, she can't eat because her jaws have turned into a pair of tentacle-like organs!). Next, she flies off to another yucca, bores into a yucca pod with her ovipositor and deposits an egg. Finally, she stuffs the pollen deep into the mouth of the pod with her "tentacles" to fertilize the yucca seeds so that they'll develop into food for her larvae. Miss one step, and the whole system breaks down. Amazing! But true.

The Useful Yucca

Several kinds of yucca are common in the canyons. With their rosettes of tough, sharp leaves and their creamy flowers, they're easy to spot.

* Yucca seeds are a favorite food of woodrats, mice, and antelope squirrels. Woodrats and deer nip off tender new leaftips.

* Buds, flowers and stalks, both cooked and raw, were eaten by both ancient and later native peoples.

*The pointed leaves were used in

A yucca needle and thread.

mending -- the sharp tip was broken off leaving the tough fiber attached -- both needle and thread for sewing. Twisted or braided together leaf fibers made tough cord and rope for construction. Cords were plaited and woven into mats and sandals (see page 18).

*The flower stalk made a good fire spindle for starting fires.

*Also called soapweed, the yucca's roots make a fair amount of cleansing suds, used by native peoples and early pioneers as shampoo.

Way Back When...
The pods of most yuccas in the redrock country split open and drop their seeds. But the banana yucca, *Yucca baccata*, relies on animals to eat its pods whole or carry them away for later eating. Paleontologists believe that during the Pleistocene (PLY-sto-seen) Era, ten thousand to two million years ago, giant ground sloths, whose fossil remains have been found in the Southwest, ate pods of the banana yucca plant and spread the seeds in their droppings.

A giant ground sloth eats yucca pods.

The Odd Couple

Who would ever expect a moth and a yucca plant to form family ties? But they do. In the spring, yucca moths gather around yucca flowers to mate.

1. After mating, the female collects pollen to take to another yucca in which she will lay her eggs.

2. The pollen ball she tucks into the flower funnel will fertilize all the sections.

Although a <u>wasp</u> may have an *ovipositor* (OH-vuh-POZ-ih-tur -- egg-laying tube) for injecting eggs into other plants or animals, it's very unusual for a moth to have one.

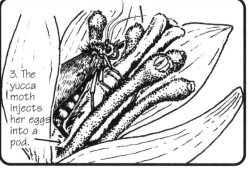

3. The yucca moth injects her eggs into a pod.

A yucca pod has several sections, and the moth inserts only one egg per section. This is a useful adaptation, for two larvae in a section might eat all the seeds so that the yucca couldn't reproduce.

4. In this cut-away view of a yucca pod, the yucca moth larva is shown eating the flat black seed discs. As autumn approaches, the larva chews through the side of the pod, drops to the ground, and spends the winter under the soil as a cocoon.
The next spring the cocoon hatches into a moth and flies to a yucca flower to find a mate and begin the cycle again.

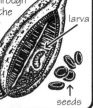

larva

seeds

Usually, only one type of moth can interact with each type of yucca, so if the moth disappears, so will that species of yucca. We discover more hidden interactions like this in nature every day, so it's important to live with our environment in ways that don't disturb the ecosystems around us.

Chapter 22. The Yucca Moth

The tiny yucca moths seemed tied to the yucca plants with invisible strings. Their lives were spent inside, on, above and between yucca plants. Some were scooped up by swifts or ash-throated flycatchers and more were eaten by bats at dusk. But enough would survive to mate and lay their eggs in the yucca pods to ensure a plentiful hatch for the next generation.

A narrow-leafed yucca grew in the canyon just below the coyote den. Its creamy blossoms rose in a glowing spire above the rosette of grey-green leaves, each leaf rimmed with silvery curls of fibers. Last year's dried flower spike, now lined with gaping brown pods, still stood beside the new flower spike, its flat black seeds long since tumbled to the sandy earth. Canyon wildlife often used the trail that ran beside the yucca, but they always stepped around the yucca respectfully, for its needle-sharp leaves could pierce the toughest skin with no trouble at all.

The evening breeze had just begun to push warm air up the canyon when a white-throated swift darted past the yucca with a rushing twitter, snatching a yucca moth that had just risen from a flower with her load of pollen. One white-throated swift with a nest full of chicks to feed; one yucca moth and all its descendants gone forever. The empty brown yucca pods rattled in the breeze, their clatter blending with a faint *zizzing* sound coming from upcanyon.

Broad-tailed Hummingbird

Selasphorus platycercus (suh-LASS-for-us   plat-ee-SIR-cuss)
Selas = "flame" *phoros* = "bearing" *platys* = "broad" *kerkos* = "tail"

The scientific name meaning "flame bearing" refers to the brilliantly colored rosy-pink gorget (GOR-jet) or bib on this little hummer's throat. Despite its name, its tail isn't *obviously* broad.

Hummingbirds are the flying jewels of the canyons, seeming much too delicate and dainty for such a dry and stony world. Listen for their zzzinging buzz!

When the spring desert wildflowers bloom, the humming-birds are there to take advantage of the nectar and the insects that also visit the flowers. The male broad-tailed hummer has a fantastic courting display, rising high into the air and diving in a deep U past a female, with a shrill screech caused by air passing through specially-shaped wing feathers. If the female is impressed, she will choose him for a mate.

The broad-tailed hummingbird produces its desert family, then flies to the cooler mountains where it raises a second brood.   It winters in western Mexico.

Zzzijjjpppp!

Picture this. You are staring with awe at the beautiful scenery when something small and fast zings past you like a bullet. You may not even see it! But keep watching, especially around the wildflowers, for the redrock canyons' airborne jewels -- the hummingbirds. If you wear something red, **you** might get "visited!" At least three kinds of hummingbirds may be found in the redrock canyons. The females all look much alike, but the males are colorful and easy to identify.

Most female and young hummingbirds of both sexes	Broad-tailed hummingbird male *Selasphorus platycercus*	Rufous hummingbird male *Selasphorus rufus*	Black-chinned hummingbird male *Archilochus alexandri*
• streaked gorget • green on cap, back, tail • white outer tail feathers	• rosy gorget • green cap, back, tail • wide, rounded tail	• brilliant orange gorget • rufous back and tail • black tailfeather tips	• black gorget • purple neck ring • green back and tail

Sip & Snap

The hummingbird's long bill is specially designed to sip nectar from long-tubed flowers like penstemons, but that doesn't stop it from snapping up insects while it's at the flower. In fact, a hummingbird will dive off a twig to catch an insect in midair.

These are some favorite hummingbird flowers.

gilia (scarlet)   penstemon (red, pink, purple)   larkspur (deep purple)

In A Very Tiny Nest

·- The little canyon hummer,
when the spring turns into summer,
knows it's time to make a very tiny nest.

·- For her mate has been a-humming,
and her eggs will soon be coming,
and she quickly has to do her very best.

·- So with catkin fluff from willows,
she creates a nest of pillows,
and with spiderwebs she binds it to a tree.

·- Her eggs hatch into nestlings,
and she feeds them all the best things
till they're big enough
to whirl their wings and flee.

·- Then they'll zip off without traces
to the high cool mountain places
where the brightly-colored
males went weeks ago.

·- There they'll sip the mountain flowers
till the shortening autumn hours
send them south and far
away from winter snow.

actual size

The nest of the broad-tailed hummingbird is 1½ to 2" across and about 1½" high. The cup is only the size of a quarter. It stretches to give the nestlings room to grow!

The Helicopter Bird

When a hummingbird flies, all you see where wings are supposed to be is a blur. Hummingbirds don't just flap their wings up and down like other birds do. To hover, they move them in a figure **8** about fifty times per second (*humans can make only about <u>one</u> movement like that per second -- you can't even count to 50 in one second!*).

When hovering, the hummingbird's wing is *upside down* on the backstroke.

Chapter 23. The Broad-tailed Hummingbird

The broad-tailed hummingbird was working late. Crickets which had spent their day in deep, cool, rock crevices had emerged to begin their evening chorus of **"kreek....kreek....kreek....kreek...."** but she wasn't ready to slow down yet.

As the white-throated swift looped upward with its mouthful of moth, the hummer buzzed the yucca, hovering in midair beside the showy yucca flowers, flaring her green, white and rufous tail into a broad fan.

In a blur of motion, she darted beneath the flowers and snapped up a yucca moth which had been swept into the air by the rush of wind from the passing swift. She perched on a spiky yucca leaf, swallowed the moth, and wiped the silvery moth scales from her long bill onto the leaf.

Then the little hummingbird took a closer look around. Along the edges of the yucca leaves curled long, strong fibers she could weave into the nest she was building in a gnarled Gambel oak some distance up the canyon. She tugged at a fiber on a live leaf, but it was firmly attached. She tried a few more, then she discovered a loose fiber on a dead leaf. On her way back

home, trailing the strong white thread, she saw some long black and white skunk hairs near a scuffed patch of sand.

She hovered over the hairs for a moment, noting the location carefully, then continued on to her tiny nest which was fastened with spiderwebs to a broad branch in the oak. The nest was two inches across and the cup was barely the size of a quarter. It was made mostly of lichens, and fluff from cottonwood and willow seeds, bound together with juniper fibers.

Lowering herself into the tiny hollow, she turned around and around to tamp down the fluff, rising up and down on blurring wings like a helicopter to adjust her position in the nest. Then, sitting in the cup, she wove the yucca fiber into the nearly-finished rim. When all the ends were tucked in tightly, she left the nest and returned to the scuffed sand to bring home the long black and white hairs she had noticed on her last trip. They would make a fine addition to her nest.

Striped Skunk

Mephitis mephitis (meh-FIT-iss meh-Fit-iss)
mephit = "bad odor" ("skunk" is from the Indian word "segankw")

Everyone knows what a skunk is -- black and white and very smelly. In fact, if you get squirted by a skunk at close range, you will have tears running down your cheeks. Your throat will sting, you will hack and cough, and you *might* upchuck. Bad stuff! The stink will stay with you like a good friend, but your "good friends" will run if you get near. Squirting range is about 12 feet (or more in a stiff breeze). You can smell such an occasion from half a mile away. Beware the skunk!

Actually, a skunk would rather not have any trouble. Unless it's surprised, a skunk usually gives plenty of warning. Its tail goes up like a flag and it springs toward you, stomping both front feet on the ground. That is body language you can't miss! If you ignore it, the skunk does a quick spin, a squirt, and you have suddenly run out of choices. Peeeuw!

In the canyon country, skunks avoid the dry desert and stay near streams and in cool canyons near water where they hunt mainly for insects in the moist earth.

Doodlebug Pits

In sandy places look for 1 - 1½ inch cone-shaped pits. Watch one for awhile and you may see a passing ant blunder over the edge and begin to slide down the slope. As you watch,

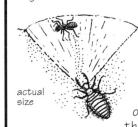

actual size

some sand flies up from the bottom of the pit, hitting the ant, which loses its balance and slips downhill. Suddenly, curved jaws reach out of the sand and pull the ant underground. Goodbye, ant! What an awful way to go!

You've been watching a doodlebug at work -- it's the larva of an insect called the antlion. The larva builds the pit, flips sand at passing insects (mostly ants), then grabs them and sucks them dry. Fortunately, doodlebugs are only half an inch long! Skunks think they taste great. (*An adult ant lion is shown on page 58.*)

Back Off!

Most animals would rather stay alive than fight -- for in nature, fighting can be fatal. Animals that have chemical defenses often wear warning signals. For instance:

*Monarch butterflies are black and orange -- eat 'em and barf.

*Poison-arrow frogs have bright colors and patterns.

(*both monarch butterflies and poison-arrow frogs contain toxic chemicals useful in human heart research*)

*Poisonous coral snakes have black, red and yellow stripes, but so do kingsnakes which are non-poisonous. (See page 64)

*Stinky skunks are easily recognized by their black and white markings.

If a predator has a bad experience with boldly patterned prey, it will avoid prey with those markings in the future -- and it may teach its young to do the same.

When it comes to skunks, that's a pretty smart idea.

If you see THIS

.....It's too late!!!

Pet Skunk? No Way!

People used to catch skunks, remove their scent glands and try to make pets of them. The problem is, these *insectivores* (in-SEK-tih-vorz -- insect eaters) are *nocturnal* (nok-TUR-null -- active at night). They keep you awake all night digging up the carpet! And if a dog attacks them, they turn their backs, fling up their tails -- and get injured or killed.

Laws have been passed in most places to make it illegal to own a skunk.

↗
Making threats is about as far as they go while in the nest!

Skunk kittens love to wrestle and play.

---

striped skunk track & scat

left hind foot
1 7/8"
left front foot

tracks are close together because the fearless skunk moves slowly

skunk scat, ½ natural size (look for insect parts)

Chapter 24. The Striped Skunk

The long black and white hairs had once grown in a skunk's tail. In fact, they were all that was left of the skunk except for some strange remains now lying on a ledge near the ancient cliff dwellings.

The skunk had been digging for doodlebugs in the soft, sandy earth of the canyon floor one moonlit night. Under a rock overhang several feet away, her four youngsters were also digging for doodlebugs. They were two months old, and she had weaned them the week before, so they were no longer growing fat on her milk. They would follow her for the rest of the summer as she hunted, copying her actions and learning the many places and ways to find insects, lizards, bird nestlings and eggs, frogs, berries, and carrion. The doodlebugs were small but easily caught.

The mother skunk was moving away down the canyon, knowing her young would follow closely on her heels, when a sudden sharp whuff of air hit her from overhead. She gave a shrill grunt, whipped her tail high and squirted out a great cloud of terrible scent. But it did not save her -- the powerful talons of a great horned owl struck hard, piercing her skull and killing her instantly. Her limp body was lifted silently into the air and carried away.

Under the rock overhang, the young skunks squealed with fear and whirled to face away from the danger, thumping their front feet in warning. Frightened and nervous, tails high and bristling, they were ready to spray -- if only they knew where to aim. But their mother and her attacker had disappeared without a trace.

They milled around frantically for a few minutes, then huddled together in a frightened ball at the back of the overhang. When their mother didn't return, they crept out onto the moonlit floor of the canyon to search for her. But soon their hunger took over and they began to forage for insects and sleeping lizards. Their mother had taught them how to care for themselves, and now their knowledge would be tested.

Great Horned Owl

Bubo virginianus (BOO-bo ver-JIN-ee-AY-nus)
Bubo = "owl"   *virginianus* = "belonging to Virginia"

If you have a chance to camp out at night in a redrock canyon, start listening just after dark. If you're lucky, you'll hear the calls of great horned owls. You may recognize the sound -- it's the owl call you usually hear on TV and movie sound-tracks when action takes place in the woods at night. It sounds like **"Whooo, hu-hoo, whoo-whooo."** An answering call will probably be higher or lower. The female owl, which is larger than the male, makes the higher call.

You probably won't hear them fly, even if they pass by quite near. The feathers on their 55" wingspread have evolved to be so silent that their prey can't hear them coming (see below right). The markings make for super camouflage.

Watch under trees and below cliffs for owl pellets. Read pages 106 and 107 for a neat owl pellet project.

Owls are major players in the ecosystem. Their steady diet of small mammals helps keep the habitat healthy.

Snack Bars

Desert great horned owls eat about 95% mammals and 5% birds, reptiles and insects. Woodrats and cottontails usually make up most of their diet, with mice, jackrabbits, skunks, and other small night creatures making most of the rest. They take fewer birds, reptiles and insects because most of those are diurnal (dye-UR-null -- daytime active) creatures.

The mouse and rat bones at left were all found in a single great horned owl pellet. (How many owl pellets can you spot on page 53?)

A few hours after eating, an owl hunches over and ejects from its beak a "pellet," two to three inches long, full of stuff it can't digest. That's our best clue about its favorite "fast foods!"

Great Horned Owlets

These chicks are one or two days old, about natural size.

The Better To See You With, M'dear

Owl eyes are awesome -- and enormous, often taking up more headroom than the brain. With these huge eyes, owls can see almost as well at night as we see on a cloudy afternoon.

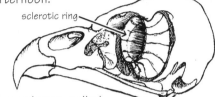

sclerotic ring

Bony plates, called the *sclerotic* (skler-AH-tik) ring surround the eye to protect it against twigs and struggling prey. They also keep wind pressure from flattening the eye and distorting the view when the owl is flying.

Owls have *binocular vision* just like people, cats and hawks -- their vision overlaps in front so that they can judge distance accurately. That's important if you are diving toward the ground at high speed!

Owls can rotate their heads 3/4 of a full circle (an owl will turn its head to watch you, but it's <u>not</u> true that you can screw off an owl's head by circling its perch!)

Silent Wings

You can hear most birds fly because their feathers are hard and smooth -- the air going past makes them whistle or whir. Owl flight feathers have velvety, fringed edges and surfaces that silence the air flowing over them.

Using Your Ears

People usually don't find their food with their ears (well, if you hear somebody munching potato chips, you might scramble to get your share). But an owl's *life* depends on its ears -- not those feathers (called "plumicorns") that stick up on its head, but the very large ears hidden under the feathers on each side of its face. By lining up its body perfectly with the sounds the prey makes, an owl can dive and catch food in dark places where even its keen eyesight is of little use.

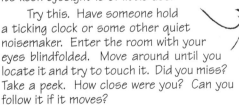

prrr...prrr...hu

Try this. Have someone hold a ticking clock or some other quiet noisemaker. Enter the room with your eyes blindfolded. Move around until you locate it and try to touch it. Did you miss? Take a peek. How close were you? Can you follow it if it moves?

Chapter 25. The Great Horned Owl

Up the cliff-dwellers' side canyon, in a nest tucked into a corner, two four-week-old owlets waited impatiently for more food. About half an hour earlier, the mother owl had brought a piñon mouse to her chicks in the hollow saucer-shaped top of the nest. The largest chick had eaten the whole thing, so the little chick was still hungry. And the big chick was ravenous *again*. One small mouse doesn't go very far with two growing owlets.

Swooping into view like a ghost in the bright moonlight, the male owl lit heavily on the edge of the nest, the mother skunk dangling from his beak. As the owlets eagerly bobbed up and down, he ripped open the skunk with his powerful hooked beak, then snipped off small bits to offer them. This time they would both have plenty to eat. When at last they were full, they closed their eyes and their beaks tight, and turned their heads away when he offered them more. He finished off the rest of the skunk himself. Neither the adult owl nor the chicks seemed to notice the terrible skunk stink that filled the air.

Contented and stuffed, the owlets polished their small beaks clean against sticks in the nest, and carefully groomed their feathers. Even though they stunk like skunks, they *looked* clean and tidy. The inside of the nest itself was clean, too, except for a few bits of cottontail fur and a snakeskin. The owlets would regularly back up to the rim of the nest and eject a big splat of poop (called "whitewash") over the edge.

A few hours after their big meal, each chick leaned out of the nest and heaved up a pellet of black and white skunk hair and fragments of bone. The pellets fell to the sandstone ledge and lay amongst the ancient potsherds and corncobs (nibbled clean by Ancestral Puebloans many centuries before) beside the old stone granary.

53

Cliff Dwellers

Dry desert air is a great preservative. In a tropical jungle, a yucca-fiber sandal would get mouldy and rot away within a month. Ancient baskets, even tucked away in a stone cave, would decay or be destroyed by insects, leaving no sign that they ever existed. Dwellings and *artifacts* (items created by ancient cultures) would disappear under fast-growing vines, shrubs and trees. That's just what happens there!

The combination of moist air, rainy seasons, swarming insects and mould are missing from the dry Southwest desert. Because of this, artifacts made centuries ago still remain -- often in nearly perfect condition -- and we are able to piece together the lives of the ancient cliff dwellers and learn how they worked and played, farmed and stored their harvests.

But our views change as we find new clues and evidence. So we base our guesses on myths, ceremonies and habits of their probable descendants, the Hopi, Zuni and Rio Grande Pueblo Indians still living in dwellings much like those in the canyons.

Many important things will never be known.

A Secret Hideout?

Why did the Ancestral Puebloans live in canyons? On ledges facing east, west or south, the cliff dwellings caught warming sunshine and protected against rain. But high on cliff walls, as many dwellings are, and as much as a mile from water and the cornfields, they must have been very inconvenient. Imagine carrying a pottery jug of water up a cliff using stone toeholds and ladders. And how about carrying up all the rocks to build the houses in the first place?

Many archaeologists believe the people were trying to conceal their dwellings, for many of them are totally hidden and can only be reached by climbing steep cliff faces and using ladders. If the villagers pulled up the ladder from a sheer cliff face, no enemy could climb up to the village.

At the time most dwellings were built, the area was in a 24-year drought, and perhaps attacks to steal food were common. If a village lost its stored food, its people might perish. That's a good enough reason to find a secret spot to live and store food for the winter. The drought may have driven the cliff dwellers from their homes, but maybe they moved for trade or religious reasons, to rejoin old friends or family, or just for a change of scenery. Who knows?

We can study what they left behind to find out *what* they did, but it is harder to know just *why.*

Digging At The Dump

Imagine digging up household garbage to learn how the neighbors live! Archaeologists do it all the time. In fact, some have been digging up modern landfills in southern Arizona to see how *modern* living habits have changed over the last few *decades*. *Peeeuw!!* Tough scientists!

Digging up an ancient dump, or *midden* (MID-'n) isn't quite so bad -- at least it doesn't stink anymore. Middens were always located close to dwellings, and what got tossed is just as interesting as what was saved.

For instance, you wouldn't save chewed gum, but the cliff dwellers apparently chewed on yucca stems and spit the used gobs onto the midden. Otherwise, we'd never have known about it -- and it tells us something about their everyday life.

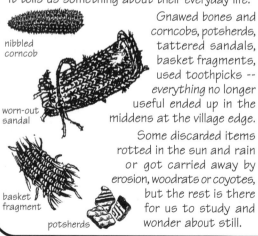

nibbled corncob

worn-out sandal

basket fragment

potsherds

Gnawed bones and corncobs, potsherds, tattered sandals, basket fragments, used toothpicks -- everything no longer useful ended up in the middens at the village edge.

Some discarded items rotted in the sun and rain or got carried away by erosion, woodrats or coyotes, but the rest is there for us to study and wonder about still.

Ancient Art

The Ancestral Puebloans made interesting rock art. Fremont Indians, living in the canyons before them, left much of their own art there, too.

Are some of the human figures that anthropologists call *anthropomorphs* supposed to be people in ceremonial clothing, or gods with strange shapes? Perhaps they are both. And what about the animals (*zoomorphs*), like the bighorn sheep with bird feet? Magic, maybe?

Are the "lizard-men" lizards, men or gods? Why were hand and moccasin shapes painted and chipped onto cliffs? Was the pawprint carved into the mud of a granary meant to frighten off woodrats? Or was it decoration? Who knows?

Always treat ancient art with respect. Touching art or carving on cliff faces destroys important scientific clues and spoils things for other visitors.

Antique Superhighways

The Ancestral Puebloans built many perfectly straight roads, up to thirty feet wide and many miles long, to connect some of their less hidden settlements. More roads are still being mapped by infrared photography. But why would people without vehicles build such roads? If you love mysteries, you've just *gotta* love the puzzle of the ancient cliff-dwelling Puebloans.

Chapter 26. The Cliff Dwellers

The granary (GRAY-ner-ee -- a storehouse for grain or harvest) was in pretty good shape, considering its age. Built nearly eight hundred years before (about the year 1200), its stone walls, once plastered with mud to keep out insects, mice and woodrats, still stood -- although its mud covering had washed away over the centuries. The stone door slab leaned against the wall where the householders had placed it before packing the last seeds into their buckskin bags and woven baskets on the day they moved away.

Some dwellings, only a few of them still whole, nestled under the overhanging cliff, although most of them had fallen away when part of the ledge broke off.

In rooms and on the ledge were things the people left behind -- broken pots, worn yucca-fiber sandals, parts from a loom, and a heavy stone metate.

Silent doorways of the ancient dwellings, built small to hold in heat during cold winter weather, waited patiently for the thud of their owners' moccasins. But the dust on the littered ledge showed no human footprints, old or new.

Below the village was a hidden midden. Buried in its depths were the remains of old bones, corncobs, broken pots, basket fragments, and obsidian flakes, chipped off while making arrowheads, spearheads and knives. Over the centuries, blowing sand had covered the midden, leaving only a smooth slope with a few broken pottery pieces scattered over the surface.

The **"whooo, hu-whoo, whooo, whooo,"** of the nesting owls echoed through crumbled stone doorways as the sky turned to flame in a fiery orange sunrise.

As the day began to warm, two gigantic black forms drifted over the canyon, casting shadows that had not been seen in this redrock canyon for eleven thousand years.

California Condor

Gymnogyps californianus (JIM-no-jips KAL-uh-for-nee-AY-nus)
Gymnos = "naked" (referring to its head)   *gyps* = "vulture"

On October 30, 1805, Lewis and Clark saw condors on the Columbia River. They called them buzzards: *"We here saw several of the large buzzards, which are the size of the largest eagle, with the under part of their wings white..."*

Wintering near Astoria, Oregon, they wrote about plants and animals they had seen so far: *"The [condor] is, we believe, the largest bird of North America. One which was taken by our hunters...[weighed] twenty-five pounds. Between the extremity of the wings the bird measured nine feet and two inches...It is not known that this bird preys upon living animals: we have seen him feeding on the remains of the whale and other fish thrown upon the coast by the violence of the waves."*

Lewis's sketch

Condors once lived from Baja California to Canada, and across the southern U.S. to Florida. They lived on the Pacific coast in the 1800's, and in California until 1985, when only nine could still be found in the wild. They were probably never numerous anywhere.

Keep Your Eyes Peeled!

Eagles, vultures, condors. They all look a lot alike when soaring at a distance -- but wait! You're in luck! No bird but the California condor has the combination of giant size, red head, and the unique pattern of white under the wings as shown below.

Note: Young condors have dark gray feathers and head until they are five years old.

golden eagle

California condor   turkey vulture

Going...Going......?

No one knows just why the condors disappeared. Perhaps the die-off of large animal herds upon which they dined in Pleistocene times 11,000 years ago was one reason. They survived until just recently near the Pacific coast on dead deer, sheep and cattle.

condor chick

Humans are the condors' main enemy. Gold miners in California in the 1850's killed them for their huge feather quills, which they filled with gold dust for safekeeping. Some livestock ranchers put out poisoned carcasses to kill predators like coyotes and eagles. Lead poisoning from eating lead bullet fragments in carcasses killed condors and other wildlife, too.

What's the Problem?

A few years ago, our government passed a law called the Endangered Species Act to make sure that animals get a fair deal. It's the only thing that has kept some wildlife from becoming extinct (disappearing from the earth forever). This law made it illegal to do anything that would kill so many animals or ruin their habitat so badly that the species might become extinct.

Some activities, like polluting and cutting down forests, have upset the balance and are changing the weather (global warming). This has made it harder for some wildlife to survive. Laws protecting the environment sometimes get in the way of what people want to do. Sometimes people try to change laws to get their own way.

If you care about wildlife, maybe you could stand up for animals and protect them, since they can't go to our government themselves to say what they need so they can stay healthy and survive!

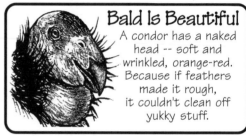

Bald Is Beautiful
A condor has a naked head -- soft and wrinkled, orange-red. Because if feathers made it rough, it couldn't clean off yukky stuff.

Flying Free At Last!

In the 1980's, there were still a few condors flying free in a tiny area of southern California. But each year their numbers became fewer as people shot them for target practice or they died from eating poisoned carcasses.

In 1987, biologists captured all that were left to save them, and started breeding them in captivity to increase their numbers. Finally, in 1996 there were enough to release and the canyon country seemed a fairly safe and appropriate place to try (see below). Since they may fly hundreds of miles in a day, you might spot one! Watch carefully, and good luck!

You may find more information on released condors at www.peregrinefund.org

Where did the Condor Wander?
How could biologists know the canyon country would be good condor habitat? In 1984, a 12,000-year-old condor skull was found at an ancient nest in a cave in the Grand Canyon. The dry air had preserved the bones perfectly.

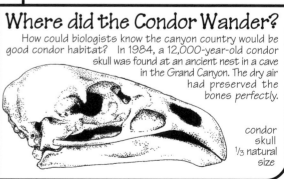

condor skull 1/3 natural size

Chapter 27. The California Condor

Although they were huge, they were still young, and the two condors soaring over Redrock Canyon were searching for their first real home. Released from a captive breeding program near the Grand Canyon, they had been exploring the vast network of canyons carved by the Colorado River and its tributaries. At night they would roost on secluded ledges, and during the warm days they would scout for food, finding an occasional deer carcass, or a dead horse or sheep from Navajo flocks.

Once condors had been common in the canyon country, nesting in south-facing caves high in the vertical sandstone cliffs. Launching from their caves with a few mighty flaps, the huge birds would spread their great wings to catch the warm, rising thermals. Then, supported by their nine-foot wingspreads, they would soar above the canyons and mesas in search of carcasses to feed on.

Quiet and wild, Redrock Canyon was an ideal place for condors. The young female's keen eyes had discovered a cave high on the face of a sheer cliff. The cave was small and sunny -- just what condors like. In fact, it was even more perfect than she thought -- lying in a pile of woodrat sticks near the rear of the cave was the skull of a condor which, thousands of years before, had also found this cave to be a perfect nest site.

After several cautious passes, the female landed on the ledge and entered the cave with growing excitement. She ducked back out to inspect the ledge. The male condor landed beside her with a rustle of black feathers and pushed past to look inside. He too liked it, and he joined her on the ledge where she had squatted down to peer over the edge. Eagles might be a problem, but no furry predator could climb to their nest on *this* cliff. Placing his head over her neck, he gently nibbled the skin on the back of her head. She turned contentedly and smoothed his soft gray throat skin with her beak. They were both hungry, and in a few minutes they would fly again, but tonight when they returned, they would be coming *home*.

Say's Phoebe

Sayornis saya (say-OR-niss SAY-uh)
Say = "named for Thomas Say, who first recorded it" *ornis* = " bird"

The name "phoebe" mimics the call of the Eastern phoebe --
"fee-bee, fee-bee." Say's phoebe is related to the eastern phoebe, but its call is really more like a wispy **"fee-weer"** or **"chu-weer."** When fluttering in the air, it says **"pippity-chee."**

You might at first mistake a Say's phoebe, with its gray back and salmon-pink breast, for a small, pale robin. But the phoebe is a flycatcher, swift and sleek, while robins are slow and sturdy -- better designed for tracking down earthworms.

If you see a bird flit from a twig to chase a fly or moth, you can be *certain* it's not a robin, because robins are too clunky to catch a flying moth! The graceful Say's phoebe flutters in the air and may even hover like a kestrel when flycatching.

If you like to explore abandoned cabins and tumble-down barns, you may find a Say's phoebe nest, because this trusting bird often nests in buildings.

Crunchy Munchies!

The diet of Say's phoebe is a checklist of the majority of the kinds of insects you can find in a desert canyon. The phoebe even picks up caterpillars, ants and millipedes on the ground.

Most items on the phoebe's menu have legs and other body parts made of chitin (KY-tin -- a hard material, a lot like fingernails) that the phoebe can't digest. So after eating, it ejects a pellet of leftovers out over the edge of the nest or roost, like an owl. If you find a pellet, you can pull it apart to find out what the phoebe has been eating.

Natural Honeypot

Myrmecocystus melliger (mur-muh-ko-SIS-tus MELL-uh-gur)

Honey ants are one of the many kinds of insects eaten by the Say's phoebe, but the phoebe never gets to eat the tastiest ones -- they stay underground!

A honey ant forager looks like an ordinary ant. It sucks up nectar and honeydew into its *crop* (a pouch in the gullet used to hold food) and carries it to the nest. There it will *regurgitate* (ree-GUR-jih-tayt -- spit up) honey to the larvae and to its nestmates. Some nestmates become storage pots for the others, eating so much honey that they can barely move.

These ants hang from the ceiling of the nest (see the picture above)and regurgitate honey for their nestmates when food becomes scarce during flowerless periods (and all winter). They may become as big as the end of your pinkie, storing eight times their own weight in honey. They'll droop from the ceiling as storage pots for the rest of their lives (*boring!*).

Maybe the Ancestral Puebloans ate honey ants as snacks -- they're <u>supposed</u> to be **delicious** (yeah, uh-huhhhh......).

Fast Food

The fluttery flight of a flycatching phoebe is very much like a bat's, and for the same reason -- it's chasing insects. Here's the path it might fly while flycatching.

How HOT Is It?

You can listen to the temperature if you know this trick: when you hear crickets chirping, count the number of chirps in 13 seconds, add 40, and the result will be very close to the Fahrenheit temperature. It works best if the cricket is the snowy tree cricket, found over much of the U.S.

(Just for fun, try this as a magic trick for your friends.)

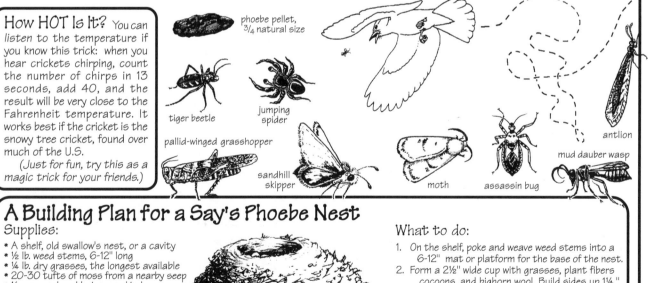

phoebe pellet, 3/4 natural size

tiger beetle

jumping spider

pallid-winged grasshopper

sandhill skipper

moth

assassin bug

antlion

mud dauber wasp

A Building Plan for a Say's Phoebe Nest

Supplies:
* A shelf, old swallow's nest, or a cavity
* ½ lb. weed stems, 6-12" long
* ¼ lb. dry grasses, the longest available
* 20-30 tufts of moss from a nearby seep
* ½ cup wool and hairs, any kind
* 150+ plant fibers (yucca, juniper, etc.)
* 6-7 empty moth cocoons
* spiderwebs

What to do:
1. On the shelf, poke and weave weed stems into a 6-12" mat or platform for the base of the nest.
2. Form a 2½" wide cup with grasses, plant fibers cocoons, and bighorn wool. Build sides up 1¼."
3. Line with moss, jackrabbit fluff, mule deer and coyote hairs. Bind together with spider webs.
4. Lay eggs and incubate. Repeat if desired.

Chapter 28. The Say's Phoebe

Without caves, alcoves, cracks and crevices, desert canyons wouldn't be very useful to wildlife. In fact, they wouldn't have been much use to the Ancestral Puebloans, either. Like most other eroding desert canyons, Redrock Canyon had many places to hide, nest, hunt, and dwell. The cliff dwellers had greatly expanded the housing in their alcove and in the high cliff across the narrow side canyon. Even after they left and the walls of many of their dwellings had partly tumbled down, the village still provided shelter in which wildlife could hide, hunt and raise families.

While building one of the rooms, a craftsman had set a wide, flat stone into the wall, pushing it to the inside of the room to make a storage shelf. On that shelf a pair of Say's phoebes had built a nest, and on the nest sat the female phoebe, incubating (INK-yew-bay-ting -- warming) four eggs. The nest was nearly twelve inches across, shallow and soft, made of dry grass, yucca fibers, fur which the nearby owls had plucked from prey, and gray fuzz from owl pellets. The phoebes were wary and quiet around the owl nest, and only visited it when seeking nesting materials.

The early morning air in the stone room was cold and the phoebe snuggled patiently in the nest keeping her eggs warm. Her mate kept watch from a singleleaf ash tree anchored in a crevice just below the alcove. His job was to supply food for his mate as she sat on the nest. It would be awhile before the air warmed enough in the small side canyon for insects to start buzzing around, so the male flew out into the sun-warmed main canyon. There he perched on a golden currant bush near the potholes and the dripping green seep, and soon darted out to snap up a dragonfly to take to his mate for breakfast.

The phoebes would spend a lot of time raising their young. As soon as their first set of chicks was ready to fledge (leave the nest), the male would teach the young ones how to flycatch, while the female would start laying and incubating a second clutch. Sitting quietly on her eggs in the cool, dusty room, the drowsy phoebe watched a patch of sunlight move over a black widow spider building its egg sac inside a broken storage pot left behind by ancient Puebloans. A large fly buzzed past on a zigzag path. Her eyes closed and she slept.

Black Widow Spider

Latrodectus mactans (lat-ro-DEK-tuss MAK-tanz)
Latro dectus = "secret biter" *mactans* = "murderous"

The black widow spider is right up there with the vampire bat, rattlesnake, scorpion and tarantula when it comes to awesome reputations of the bad kind. But far more people die of honeybee stings than spider bites.

A black widow is timid. It isn't going to sneak into your sleeping bag at night for a snack. It wants *nothing* to do with you, you gigantic monster! In fact, the black widow is hard to get a good look at, because it zips out of sight in its web if you try to get a close-up peek. It may live for a year or more.

The female black widow is a beautiful spider, with her polished black body and legs and the red pattern on her abdomen. The male has black and white zebra stripes, and bulbous pedipalps (PEDDI-palps -- the "feelers" next to its mouth) in which it carries sperm for the female black widow during mating. Any spider with bulbous front feelers is male.

Making Spider Silk

Spider silk is miraculous stuff. A spider can decide to spin sticky or non-sticky web by choosing which of her web nozzles or spinnerets to use. This is important because snare webs should be sticky, while the spider's living quarters and egg sacs should *not*.

The spinnerets are located at the rear of the spider's abdomen, within easy reach of its hind legs, which are lined and tipped with tiny combs to help it grasp the silk. The black widow's silk is *ten times as strong as steel*. Small mice have been caught in black widow spider webs.

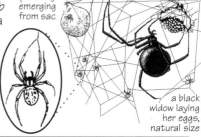

combs on rear legs →

Silk is made by spinnerets on abdomen

A Rotten Reputation

Since black widows are often found around our houses, it may seem odd to find them out in the wild canyon country, too. Their relatives, commonly called "house spiders" look similar, and people mistake them for black widows and mash them. But house spiders are browner and smaller, and they don't have the red "hourglass" markings on their undersides.

house spider
Theridion species
natural size

The female's glossy black body may be nearly 3/8" wide (see below). The red abdominal marking is usually obvious and may look like one of these → ▯ ⋈ ⋈ ⊗ 吕

The male is about one-fourth her size, and has beautiful brown (or black) and cream zebra markings and a yellow (or cream) hourglass.

The female may eat the male after mating if she's hungry -- but this is true of many spiders, although only the black widow has gotten the rotten reputation.

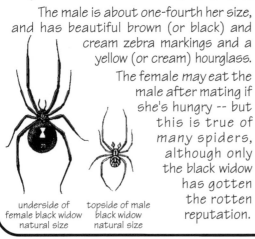

underside of female black widow natural size

topside of male black widow natural size

Family Matters

Look in a black widow web and you may see a cream-colored ball a little bigger than a pea. Is it an egg? No -- its a bag, or sac, full of 300 to 500 eggs! When a black widow has eggs to lay, she weaves a ¼" deep cup of non-sticky web. Then she inserts her abdomen into the cup and deposits her eggs inside. She closes the cup by weaving a dome over the eggs. The eggs hatch in two to four weeks, and some spiderlings eat each other inside the sac. As they grow, they molt (split open the old skin and crawl out). Then they chew an opening in the sac and exit. The spotty babies hang around in mom's web for a few days wrapping and eating anything tiny that hits the web, then they climb onto a twig or stone, spin out a long strand of silk, and let a breeze carry them away to a new home. If they don't leave, she'll EAT them.

spiderlings emerging from sac

This is a close-up of a hatchling. ↗ Females get more dark markings with every molt until their backs are all black. Males remain spotted.

a black widow laying her eggs, natural size

Live and Let Live

Since the black widow spider IS poisonous enough to kill you (about 4% of the people who are bitten die), here are some spider-wise DO's and DONT'S for visitors to the canyon country:

* **don't stick your fingers into dark holes**
* **avoid super-strong, stretchy spiderwebs**
* **check cave ceilings before entering**
* **don't kill spiders -- avoid them**

Black widow spiders are an important part of the canyon ecosystem -- one spider may eat 2,000 insects during a lifetime. They generally won't bother you if you don't bother them.

Chapter 29. The Black Widow Spider

The spider, sleek and shiny black, had strung her web inside a beautifully painted but broken pot which the Ancestral Puebloans had left behind when they moved. Made with a round bottom, it had been placed on a woven yucca-leaf pot-rest ring to hold it upright. The tattered ring had collapsed over the centuries, tilting the broken pot to one side. The hollow darkness made a perfect spider home.

The black widow spider had been growing fatter and rounder over the last few weeks as eggs inside her developed and enlarged. Now she hung upside-down in her web inside the pot and started spinning and looping a special non-sticky web with her hindmost pair of legs and spinnerets. When she had finished weaving a cream-colored pea-sized cup, she rested for awhile, then inserted the tip of her abdomen into the sac and started laying tiny yellow eggs. Slightly sticky, they clung

together in a clump as she wove the sac shut around them. Then she cut the sac loose from the web, hooked the claws of a hind foot into loose webbing at the small end and dragged it along behind her like a gigantic purse.

Empty of eggs now, she was shrunken and wrinkled, exhausted and hungry. Guarding her egg sac, she began to spin a fresh web to trap passing insects. The sucked-dry corpses of moths and crickets wrapped in silk on the stone floor beneath the web showed what she usually ate.

A black widow spider is extremely cautious and shy, which is one reason she lives so long. She scrambles up into her funnel-shaped nest when she sees danger approaching. Unfortunately for this busy black widow, the new egg sac was blocking her view when a hungry canyon wren flew past and noticed her.

61

Canyon Wren

Catherpes mexicanus (kuh-THER-peez   mek-sih-KAY-nuss)
Catherpes = "to creep down"   *mexicanus* = "belonging to Mexico"

The canyon wren spends a lot of its time creeping into dark cracks and behind rocks and boulders looking for its favorite food -- insects, spiders and their relatives. That's how it got its scientific name. Sometimes people mistake a canyon wren for a mouse at first because they don't expect to see a bird creeping under and behind rocks.

This lovely little bird is the color of the redrock canyons, and its throat and chest are pure white. Like other wrens, it flicks and bobs its tail -- up slowly and down very quickly -- which makes it easy to identify from a distance (the rock wren bobs, too, but it is more gray with a streaky throat, and its song is WAY different (see page 26).

Almost certainly, though, your first experience with a canyon wren will be with your ears. Just listen in a canyon for a "laughing" bird and it's likely to be a canyon wren.

or, Cheep, Cheep!

Did you ever try to describe a bird song to someone? You probably used words like "chirp, cheep, tweedle," and you probably made your voice go up and down the way the bird's did. But you probably didn't sound much like the bird (hope that doesn't hurt your feelings)!

Ornithologists (people who study birds) use sonogram (SAH-no-gram) equipment to record bird songs. On a sonogram you can see song pattern, tempo, volume, range, and quality, although it takes some practice.*

Here is a word description of the canyon wren's call (taken from several different sources): --a clear, loud, silvery whistle lilting down the scale, starting out with single, sharp notes, then becoming slower, each note picking up at the end, sounding like 'tooey, tooey, tooey' or 'tew, tew, tew.' You might be able to recognize a canyon wren song from that description. A sonogram lets you _see_ the pattern. Every clue helps!

top note on the piano
3rd C above middle C
2nd C above middle C
1st C above middle C
middle C on piano

A sonogram of 2½ seconds of the canyon wren's call looks like this (check it out on a piano).

Whistling for the dog looks like this.

It's Fine To Be Flat

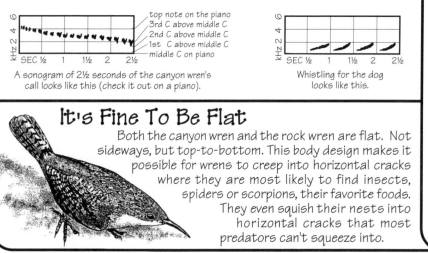

Both the canyon wren and the rock wren are flat. Not sideways, but top-to-bottom. This body design makes it possible for wrens to creep into horizontal cracks where they are most likely to find insects, spiders or scorpions, their favorite foods. They even squish their nests into horizontal cracks that most predators can't squeeze into.

*See *A Guide to Field Identification, Birds of North America.* by Robbins, Bruun and Zim; published by Golden Press (pages 14 and 15) for a really excellent guide to reading a sonogram.

Scorpion Tales

People love to scare themselves -- that's why horror movies are so popular. Scorpions you'd meet in the canyon country aren't nearly as deadly as people like to think (though the Giant Hairy Scorpion, not shown here, may be a scary 3-5" long). It is dark with a yellowish tail.

The only really dangerous redrock country scorpion (known to have caused death to infants and small children) is the bark scorpion (see below). The rest of them will cause some wasp-sting-type pain if they zap you. The scorpions below are life size.

Centruroides exilicauda
formerly known as
C. *sculpturatus*
straw-colored
slender body
narrow tail
deadly poison
bad guy
2¼ - 2¾"

Vejovis spinigeris→
greenish-yellow or straw-colored
chunky body, thick tail, painful sting
not-so-bad guy   2 - 3"

If you see a slim, streamlined scorpion just over 2" long, **look out.**

If it is chunky and/or larger, admire it but don't get too close. Like the black widow, scorpions are an important part of the food chain, so **don't kill them -- avoid them.** When camping, ALWAYS shake out shoes and clothes before dressing.

Oasis (oh-AY-sis)

An oasis is a moist green spot in a desert. If the moisture oozes from a cliff, it is called a seep. Here are some plants you might find at a seep.

small-flowered columbine
Aquilegia micrantha

Eastwood monkey-flower
Mimulus eastwoodii

maidenhair fern
Adiantum capillus-veneris

Chapter 30. The Canyon Wren

Looking for food for her hungry chicks, the canyon wren made a quick aerial U-turn to check out the movement inside the broken pot. Spotting the big spider, she tried to land on the edge of the pot so that she could reach in and spear it with her long, curved bill. But a strand of the strong web silk

caught the tip of her wing, flipping her off balance. The wren pinwheeled into the trash beside the pot while the shiny black spider scrambled up out of reach in her funnel-nest, dragging her egg sac behind her.

The Say's phoebe watched the entertainment from her warm nest on the shelf as the canyon wren fought free of the sticky web with muffled, angry squeaks.

Rumpled and flustered, the wren flew out of the ruins. Landing on a boulder below the ledge, she groomed her feathers back into order, and wiped her bill clean against the orange sandstone. Bobbing and flicking her tail, she began to pry up rocks and peer beneath. Under the fifth rock, she found a scorpion. She quickly grabbed it and bashed it against the ground to kill it and break off its poisonous tail-tip. Then she carried it to the seep in the main canyon where her newly-fledged youngsters were making their first flights and crash-landings as they waited for her to return with food.

The seep was a green oasis where water dripped down the face of the rock and filled small hollows, or potholes in the redrock sandstone with pools of life-giving water. In late summer the seep would sometimes dry up, and the mud would crack and bake in the smaller potholes. But just now, fed by the dripping seep and a cloudburst the week before, all the potholes were brimming. The wren landed on a flat fossil sand dune (see page 5) and sang past her mouthful of scorpion *"Ti-ti-ti-tui-tui-tui-tui-too."*

Within seconds she was surrounded by her four fledglings, crouching and fluffing their feathers and begging for the scorpion. She poked it into the widest-open mouth, then flew off to find food for the rest of her chicks.

Striped Whipsnake

Masticophis taeniatus (mass-tih-KO-fus   tay-nee-AY-tus)
Masti = "whip" *ophi* = "serpent" *taenia* = "ribbon or band"

When hiking in the canyon country, it's a good idea to keep an eye out for snakes, especially if you are climbing around on rocks or looking into caves or crevices. But although it's wise to be careful, there's no need to be scared to death! If you ask people who actually live there, they'll probably tell you that they seldom see snakes of any kind, venomous (VEN-uh-muss -- poisonous) or non-venomous.

The striped whipsnake is one of the non-venomous kind, but you'll have to be sharp-eyed to get a look, because it is speedy, shy and very alert. It is an important member of the ecosystem, and helps keep things in balance by eating lizards, other snakes and small mammals. It won't chase you.

If you spot a lo-o-o-o-ng (up to 5 feet), slim, brown-and-cream-striped snake traveling head-up and peering from side to side, it's probably a striped whipsnake.

How Do You Eat Somebody Bigger Than You?

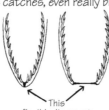

quadrate bone

eye opening

claw-like teeth hold prey

It's not easy to hold onto prey when you have no legs or claws, so a snake needs to swallow *whatever* it catches, even really big stuff. Luckily, a snake's lower jaw is attached to a special movable bone called a quadrate (KWAW-drayt), which allows the back of the jaw to drop down and swing wide.

Hey, it works -- now, what's for lunch?

This flexible ligament connects the front tips of the lower jawbones. It stretches like a rubber band to let the lower jaw spread wider.

Is It Poisonous?

If you DO find a snake (see box at left) it's good to know if it is dangerous. How can you tell? For starters, the only venomous snakes in the canyon country are rattlesnakes.

CORAL SNAKES are poisonous, but they are NOT found in the Colorado Plateau desert canyons. They live in the Southeastern U.S. and in southern Arizona. They are banded red, yellow (or white) and black. See below.

coral snake
yellow
red
red
black
kingsnake

A snake with these colors in the canyon country may be a harmless milk snake, longnose or kingsnake. This poem tells which stripe colors are next to each other:

> *Red by yellow, kill a fellow.* (coral snake)
> *Red by black, poison lack.* (harmless snake)

RATTLESNAKES have big, bulgy jaws. The markings of many snakes, especially the gopher snake, resemble the rattlesnake's,

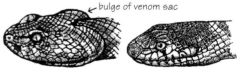

← bulge of venom sac

rattlesnake   gopher or bull snake

so instead of markings, look for the wide, arrowhead-shaped head. The bulges outline the venom sacs under the skin!

OTHER CANYON COUNTRY SNAKES are not venomous, but MOST snakes will bite if frightened, so don't try to catch them or hurt them. Just watch from a distance.

Snake Bit

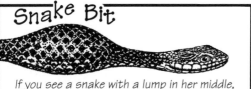

*If you see a snake with a lump in her middle, that's dinner that's in her, not fat.
She may not have had any dinner all winter, and maybe that lump is a rat.*

The Belly Walkers

Ever wonder how snakes move? It isn't easy. Just **try** squirming across the lawn on your belly with your hands grasped behind your back and your legs tight together (no pushing with your toes!). Now, catch and eat a mouse! Good luck!

the 'concertina method' viewed from above

1. press lift head forward
2.
3. lift tail forward press
4.
5. repeat...

Whipsnakes use the 'concertina method' (a concertina is an accordian) to move. They can even climb trees by pressing a loop of the body partly around the trunk while other parts are lifting and moving up. Rows of scales provide traction. Other snakes like boas and sidewinders use different methods to travel.

traveling in dust →   snake track & scat   snake scat ½ natural size

Chapter 31. The Striped Whipsnake

The mother wren delivered food every few minutes, but the young wrens also looked for their own tidbits. Late that afternoon, one little wren heard a swishing of sand behind a boulder near the seep. Hopping closer, he cocked his head to one side, then boldly fluttered to the top of the rock to get a better look.

Suddenly he had a *very good* view -- much better than he wanted. He had landed just a few inches above a startled striped whipsnake. Seeing a flutter of movement, the five-foot-long snake jerked into a defensive coil, hissing loudly and ready to strike. The astonished and frightened wren chick somersaulted backward off the rock in his haste to escape, disappearing from the snake's view before she could see what had "attacked" her. The snake hissed again, her coils tightening, but the mysterious "foe" didn't come back over the top of the rock.

The wren chick was, in fact, gone. Scrambling into the air, he fluttered wildly across the biggest pothole and crash-landed in a bush, fearful and trembling. He'd never seen a snake before, but he knew instinctively that he had just escaped from something terrible. He would be more cautious in the future.

Unwinding silently, the whipsnake rippled back out of sight into the vegetation that sucked moisture from the dunes around the seep.

Short-horned Lizard

Phrynosoma douglassii (frih-NO-suh-muh duh-GLASS-ee-i)
Phryno = "toad" *soma* = "body" *douglassii* = "named for Douglas"

Horned lizards, also called horned toads, aren't toads at all (although their scientific name is "toad-body"). Real toads are moist amphibians, and start out as tadpoles in a pool of water. Short-horned lizards are scaly reptiles and give birth to tiny lively babies on dry land (most lizards -- even all other horned lizards -- lay eggs). And even though they do look a bit like toads, they don't hop or act like toads.

Baby horned lizards may be eaten by birds, snakes and other lizards, but the adults puff up and poke their attackers with their sharp horns if caught. Predators have been found dead with adult horned lizards caught in their throats (ouch!).

"Horny toads" used to be popular as pets and were collected almost to extinction for the pet trade. In many states, they're now a protected species -- so if you find one, it's okay to look, but don't touch.

Our Native Anteater

Horned lizards squat next to anthills and pick off ants with their soft, pink tongues. Chemicals in their blood protect them from the ants' formic acid. These harvester ants are taking seeds and leaves back to their anthill for later meals.

Horned Wizard!

You're watching a pale pink horned lizard licking up ants on the pale pink sand when the sun goes behind a cloud. You watch the lizard slowly turn reddish brown!

A horned lizard takes on the color of the soil where it lives. But when it gets hot, it turns a lighter shade of that color (which helps it cool off). When it gets too cool, it turns darker to warm up again. If the temperature *really* rises, it digs down under the sand to cool off.

A Lizard Portrait

Horned lizards appear as designs on Ancestral Puebloan rock art and pottery. Navajos use them in sand paintings and rugs to symbolize good luck.

Horned lizard designs have been found on ancient ladles.

Mountain or Desert?

A horned lizard on the Colorado Plateau may be a mountain short-horned lizard or a desert horned lizard, *Phrynosoma platyrhinos* ("flat-nose"). Which is the one in the story?

← Notice the differences?

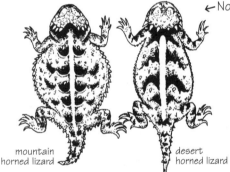

mountain horned lizard   desert horned lizard

Thorny Devil Look-Alike

In the dry deserts of Australia lives the *thorny devil*, a lizard that's totally unrelated to our American horned lizards, but is amazingly similar. It even eats ants and changes skin color like our horned lizards. They share another amazing trait -- both drink rain that runs down grooves between their scales and into their mouths. These traits show *convergent evolution* -- similar environmental pressures resulting in similar organisms (plants or animals) that converge or "come together" on the solution to a problem.

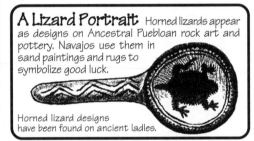

Moloch horribilis
(MOLL-uck hor-IB-ul-uss)

Over Easy

Most horned lizards lay up to 25 eggs in a hole and let the sun's heat incubate them. Egg-layers are **oviparous** (oh-VIP-ur-uss).

But the short-horned lizard lives in colder places where the sun's heat might not incubate the eggs. So she keeps them in her body until they're ready to hatch -- that's called being **ovoviviparous** (oh-voh-vy-VIP-ur-uss). The babies pop out in transparent sacs that look like plastic bags, and kick their way free, already able to look after themselves. Animals born *without eggshells* are said to be **viviparous** (vy-VIP-ur-uss). You're one.

1"

Does Squirting Blood Scare Ya?

If you grabbed a lizard and it squirted **blood** at you, would you be startled enough to drop it? A horned lizard can squirt blood from its eyes six to seven feet (freaky, huh?) and this seems to frighten off coyotes and foxes. It squirts by quickly tightening neck muscles around its jugular veins.

Then tiny blood vessels in its head fill with pressurized blood until they burst, and blood squirts out through the membranes around its eyes.

To shed its skin, it tightens the same muscles -- but more slowly -- swelling up its head until the skin splits and flakes away around all the "horns." It would NEVER get that old skin off otherwise.

Chapter 32. The Short-horned Lizard

The late afternoon air around the seep was pulsing with the shrill buzz of cicadas as the short-horned lizard snapped up harvester ants entering and leaving their anthill. Around her were seventeen tiny short-horned lizard babies, still soft and tender from birth earlier that day. They hadn't eaten anything yet -- the red ants were too big for them to swallow. Soon they would wander off, seeking tiny black ants and other mini-prey. If they didn't get eaten first.

The lizard family froze in sudden alarm as the whipsnake, retreating from her wren "attack" slid swiftly past. They should have stayed motionless -- their coloring, pinkish-grey-with-black-speckles, made them almost invisible. But the snake brushed against two of the babies and in a frenzy of motion, most of the lizard family disappeared beneath a layer of loose sand by instinctively jerking their heads and bodies from side to side and windmilling the sand with their feet. This was the first time the babies had tried to dig in, and some of them were still partly visible when they stopped moving. Still, most of them blended well with the pink sand.

As the shower of sand landed on her shining scales, the snake stopped abruptly and swung her head around. One tiny horned lizard had been perched on a slab of dark red rock as the snake came by, and even though it had paddled furiously with all four feet it had not been able to cover itself with sand. It was clearly visible to the snake, and she didn't hesitate -- her open mouth plunged out and down, and the newborn lizard was soon only a lump in her slim neck. Its pointed scales were still small and blunt, and it went down smoothly.

The mother lizard, like all horned lizards, wasn't concerned about the fate of her babies. They would have to make it through life on their own. She WAS frightened for herself, though, and as the sand settled over her she lay perfectly still, eyes wide, watching as the satisfied whipsnake rippled away past the anthill through the clumps of graceful needle-and-thread grass.

Although digging down under the sand is a good way to disappear, it can have some drawbacks, too. Covered with sand, the horned lizards were invisible to the mule deer watchfully picking its way through the shrubby clumps of Mormon tea to the potholes for a drink. The deer was alert for big danger -- coyote, cougar or perhaps a hungry bobcat -- not for a buried four-inch lizard and sixteen tiny babies.

Mule Deer

Odocoileus hemionus (oh-doh-KOY-lee-uss hem-ee-OH-nuss)
Odous = "tooth"   *koilos* = "hollow"   *hemionos* = "mule"

The mule deer's odd scientific name refers to its tooth shape and the fact that its ears are the size of a mule's -- it isn't *really* a "hollow-toothed mule." The blacktail deer in the northwestern U.S. is a subspecies of the mule deer, or "muley."

Watch for mule deer at dawn and dusk, because this is when they emerge from their sleeping spots to browse. Grazers, like bighorn sheep, eat mostly grass; but deer nibble leaves and tender twigs (called "browse") from shrubby plants and trees. Because they eat different things, deer and bighorn both have plenty to eat even though they share the same desert territory.

In November and December, the bucks fight each other to breed with the does. After mating, the bucks gather into bachelor herds for the winter, while the does form their own herds. Pregnant does leave the herd briefly in spring to have their fawns. A mule deer usually lives about ten years.

No Adoption Necessary

You'd think a mother deer would keep her baby close to her to protect it from danger. But by hiding it in brush or grass, she may keep it from being noticed at all (this is why people think they've found "abandoned" fawns).

A newborn fawn is small -- only 12 - 14" high and 5 - 7 lbs -- and has a heavily spotted "camouflage coat" to break up its outline. For the first week or so, the fawn has no scent, so a passing coyote probably won't notice the fawn, huddled flat and motionless against the ground. The doe stays nearby and comes to nurse her fawn eight or ten times every twenty-four hours. As soon as the fawn can run easily (usually three weeks older and several inches taller) both doe and fawn rejoin the herd. By fall, it will no longer need milk.

June 15

Deer Differences

It's not likely that you'll see mule deer and our other American deer, the whitetail deer, together. The whitetail sticks to moist forests and meadows, while the mule deer prefers dry woods, brush, and open spaces. Still, where these two habitats meet, look for differences in **antlers, ears, rumps** and **scent glands.** Compare them below.

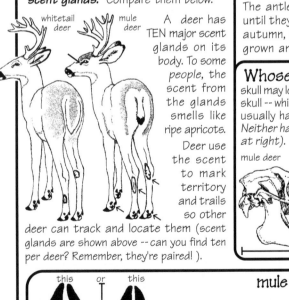

whitetail deer   mule deer

A deer has TEN major scent glands on its body. To some people, the scent from the glands smells like ripe apricots.

Deer use the scent to mark territory and trails so other deer can track and locate them (scent glands are shown above -- can you find ten per deer? Remember, they're paired!).

Soft, Warm & FUZZY?

Fuzzy knobs appear on the buck's forehead in March. Soft and warm, they are formed of semi-hard bone, surrounded and nourished by blood vessels, and covered with skin. These are the deer's antlers. By June they will be full size. The deer is *"in velvet."*

An old buck's antlers have many branches, or tines, but a yearling has only single tines, called spikes. The antlers grow all summer. The deer moves carefully -- until they harden, a sharp blow will damage an antler. In autumn, the velvety coverings shrink and peel off the full-grown antlers as the buck rubs them against trees and branches, preparing to fight other bucks for the does. When breeding season is over, the antlers fall off and are eaten by rodents. That's why you don't find many antlers lying around.

The shaded area shows the fully formed antler inside the velvet

May 1
April 1

Whose Skull?
A doe mule deer skull may look a bit like a domestic sheep skull -- which is shorter and heavier, and usually has a convex (arched) profile. Neither has upper front teeth (see box at right).

mule deer

8 -10"

domestic sheep

10 - 12"

Toothless?
Deer and sheep don't have upper front teeth. The tongue presses a twig or leaf against a tough fleshy pad where you'd expect to find upper incisors, then sharp lower front teeth slice up through the food until they meet the pad. Twigs nibbled by deer have frayed edges -- rabbits cut clean.

cutaway view
pad   nose
tongue   twig
lower jaw

CHOM

this   or   this
3¼"

mule deer track & scat

. . 20 - 24" . .

walking in dust →   back hoofprint may overlay front hoofprint

deer scat, natural size. pellets may be stuck together if browse is moist and tender

Chapter 33. The Mule Deer

When the deer walked right through the middle of the buried lizard family, the lizards lost their cool. Erupting from hiding in a shower of sand, they streaked off in all directions looking for safer shelter. The astonished deer leaped straight up with an explosive snort like ripping silk, making a sideways bound which ended in the deep sand below the potholes. After a few leaps, the buck realized he wasn't being chased, and he stopped, huge ears flipping back and forth to listen for danger. He stared nervously back at the anthill. The white hairs on his rump were raised and bristling with alarm.

Cicadas, which had fallen silent during the ruckus, started buzzing again and crickets began to tune up for their evening concert. The horned lizards were now hidden under bushes and rocks, and the deer could see nothing suspicious. He sniffed the air carefully, smelling nothing unusual. Finally, one step at a time, he approached the potholes. Every few feet he stopped, shook his velvet antlers, snorted sharply and stamped a hoof. But nothing else moved on the brushy flats around the potholes. The buck finally reached the smallest pothole and lowered his head to drink. He sipped for a long time, the water filling out the hollows on his sides, then he lifted his dripping muzzle. He sniffed the air deeply for danger, then stepped across a line of ancient dinosaur tracks in the sandstone and continued on his way down the canyon to browse on willows near the beaver pond.

Great Basin Spadefoot Toad

Scaphiopus intermontanus (skaf-ee-OH-pus in-tur-mon-TAY-nus)
Scaphiopus = "digger"   *intermontana* = "between the mountains"

Meet the little spadefoot toad. Its lifestyle is really weird! The spadefoot toad lays its eggs in fast-drying puddles, so the eggs must hatch pronto -- in nine to seventy-two hours. In as few as ten days, they *metamorphose* (met-uh-MOR-fohs -- transform) into toads, then leave the pool in a large group. Other toads take weeks to mature. Bullfrogs take two years!

Spadefoot toads do a lot of things together. The tadpoles wag their tails together to stir up the pothole's mud and swirl decayed vegetation up into the water where they can eat it.

Adult males gather together in pools to croak, because the louder they sing, the more females they can attract.

But if food runs out in the tadpoles' pool, togetherness and being nice won't keep them alive -- so the bigger tadpoles eat their smaller classmates. That way at least **some** tadpoles survive to make more spadefoot toads. (See page 71.)

Stone Pool On A Fossil Beach

Sandstone is made of grains of sand cemented together by water, minerals, heat and pressure over millions of years. A desert pothole is a hollow place carved into a sandstone surface by floods, rain or wind -- or all three.

Rain, usually slightly acid, dissolves weaker areas of the "cement," loosening the sand grains -- which the wind then blows away. Once started, a hollow gets bigger and bigger. Sometimes it gets colonized by the organisms that form cryptobiotic soil (see page 4). But if it fills with rain or floodwater, odd things start to happen!

a dried-up pothole
with curls of mud

A Desert "Tidepool"
A pothole is sort of like an ocean tidepool -- without the tide. When rain fills the pool, you may find some or all of the critters shown at right -- or you may find none of them. But how could **anything** get there? Well, things fly or float in on the wind or flood, or come as eggs stuck to birds' feet. If the pothole dries up, insects fly away. Snails burrow deep into the mud, which arrived by wind or flood. Shrimps and other dwellers lay eggs, then die. Tadpoles become toads. The dried mud in the pothole may heat up to 140° on a hot day, so the buried creatures, eggs and larvae must be able to take the heat or they'll be toast.

The cracked mud in the bottom of a dry pothole is full of these tough little eggs, larvae, pupae and snails waiting for the next good rain, when they'll emerge and start all over again. Don't step on them or disturb their pothole habitat -- they have enough problems!

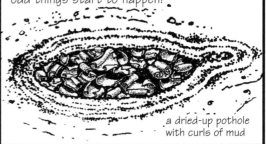

1. tadpole shrimp -- 1"
2. spadefoot toad tadpoles -- 1/8" at hatching, 3/8" or more when they leave the pothole
3. whirligig beetle -- 1/2"
4. fairy shrimp with egg mass -- 1"
5. backswimmer -- 1/2" or more
6. horsehair worm -- 10" or more
7. clam shrimp -- 1/2"
8. cranefly larva -- 1 1/2"
9. snail -- 1/2"
10. mosquito larva -- 1/2"

Blue Crows?
If you see what seem to be big blue crows playing hopscotch in the sand dunes, try to get a closer look. They're piñon jays, moving in loose flocks, with the ones at the rear flying to the front to hunt for piñon nuts, seeds, tadpoles, beetles and insects, only to be "leapfrogged" by others behind them.

"QUEK! QUEK! QUEK!" means one of them found something good to share!

young piñon jay

If you see a bird with soft, pink "lips," it's a fledgling.

jay track, 1/2 natural size

Corkscrew Toad

Tog or Froad?
The spadefoot is not your average toad. After it leaves its birth-pond, it's strictly a dry-land critter (except when mating). That's normal toad behavior. But it has smooth skin -- that's frog stuff. Also, this 1½ - 2" toad has unique vertical eye pupils like a cat's and a bump like a fingernail clipping on the sole of each hind foot for digging. Definitely not standard equipment. Listen for its "Waa-waa-waa" mating calls after a cloudburst.

A spadefoot (natural size) digs in.

toad track   & scat

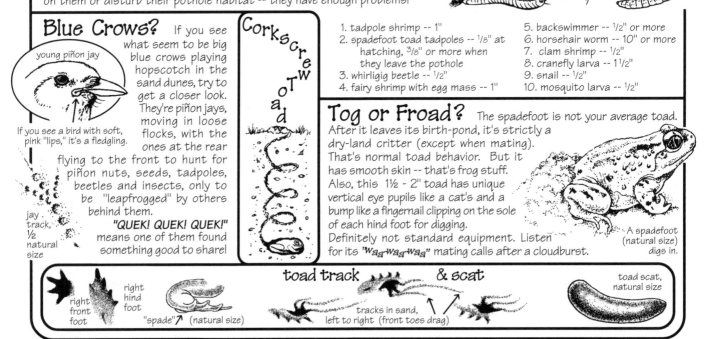

right front foot
right hind foot
"spade" (natural size)
tracks in sand, left to right (front toes drag)
toad scat, natural size

(What do you call the toad's spade? A toads"tool," of course! Toadstool, get it?)

Chapter 34. The Great Basin Spadefoot Toad

In the smallest pothole, twenty-seven spadefoot toad tadpoles, looking like tiny black olives, clustered in the center of the pothole while the deer sucked up an alarming amount of their watery home.

The pool had become smaller and shallower each day as the water was drunk by wildlife and evaporated in the hot desert air. Some years the entire hatch of tadpoles might die in the drying mud, for tadpoles must turn into toads before they can leave their pool. These tadpoles still had tails but they also had legs. Now, sixteen days after being laid as eggs, they were ready to transform into toads.

As the evening light began to fade, an urgent new feeling tugged at them. Suddenly, they all began to crawl together out over the ring of dried mud around the pothole and onto the sandstone. The still-warm air sucked moisture from their wet skins and the rough rock scraped their tender bellies.

The dry air and big, empty sky made them very nervous, and they hopped hastily toward the dark shadow of some spiky blackbrush growing a few feet from the edge of the pothole, tumbling headfirst into the shallow fossil dinosaur tracks and tripping over their tails in their rush to reach shelter.

But they had been discovered. The excited *"QUEK! QUEK!"* of a piñon jay brought the rest of the flock, fifteen hungry birds, streaking across the sand dunes toward the wiggly feast of toadlets. The first three jays gulped down several toadlets, but the rest escaped to safety under the thorny twigs.

The lucky survivors huddled motionless for nearly half an hour in the spiky tangle until the jays left. In that short time their tails became almost entirely absorbed into their bodies. They emerged from cover, wide-eyed, to learn how to live in this strange, new world.

They would feed on ants and beetles every night. Each dawn they would dig down through the dry sand, turning in jerky backward spirals and kicking sideways with the fingernail-like "spades" on their hind feet to corkscrew down to moist sand -- as deep as twelve feet.

Growing hungry, they would claw their way to the surface, eat and drink, grow and shed their skins, then spiral back down into darkness. There they would stop breathing, absorbing oxygen only through their skins. If the earth baked so hard they couldn't emerge, they might have to wait for weeks or months until rain softened the sand. But most would survive.

With next summer's first heavy cloudburst, they would gather once more in a pothole. The canyon would echo with the males' loud, raspy *"Waa-waa-waa-waa-waa!"* and the females would arrive hop by hop, from as far as a mile away to mate and lay eggs for the next generation of spadefoot toads.

Yuma Myotis Bat

Myotis yumanensis (my-OH-tiss yew-muh-NEN-sis)
Myotis = "mouse ear" *yumanensis* = "belonging to Yuma (Arizona)"

The Yuma myotis is found all over the west and is one of the commonest and most ordinary bats in the canyon country. Its smallish body is 3 to 3¾" from nose to tail tip. It has short brown fur and no special features. A fast flyer, it often hangs around *riparian* (rih-PAIR-ee-un -- marsh, pond or streambank) areas hunting with a zig-zag pattern close to the water surface. Most other species of bats found in the desert tend to flutter higher overhead in drier areas.

In summer, the males usually roost alone in crevices or behind rock flakes, while the females roost in large colonies in caves or mines with their young -- up to 5,000 in a roost. No one knows where Yuma myotis bats spend the winter.

Myotis bats are insectivorous, eating moths, flies, beetles, and water insects like caddis flies, craneflies, midges and mosquitoes (YES!). Watch for them from early evening till dark.

Bat Habits....
Bats live strange lives that we can barely imagine. Think of all the things they do that we can't:

* flying -- looping and fluttering through the air
* echolocation (eh-ko-lo-KAY-shun) -- using reflected sound to find prey
* maneuvering in total darkness -- hmmm. that could be handy....
* hibernation -- winter shut-down to stay alive when food is unavailable
* diurnation (die-ur-NAY-shun) -- daytime slow-down to save energy
* hanging around upside down -- well, every lifestyle has its down-side

Because they have such energy-conserving lifestyles, bats may live up to twenty years. This is very unusual in the animal kingdom, because small animals usually have short life spans. A mouse, for instance, is old at 1½ years. But since bats spend most of their lives with their systems shut down (hibernation all winter and diurnation every day all summer) and being active only two to four hours out of twenty-four, their bodies simply last longer.

Insect "Fuzz Buster"

Some moths can tune in on a bat's sonar frequency (see page 100).

Their "Fuzz Buster" goes off and they slam on the brakes, loop, reverse, drop like a rock -- whatever it takes to escape. Some moths can actually jam a bat's sonar with their own clicks! It doesn't always work, but it helps a moth escape often enough to be worth trying!

What About Rabies?

Can you get rabies (RAY-beez -- a disease) from bats? Possibly! But you can also get it from other mammals -- dogs, cats, raccoons, and (are you ready for this?) PEOPLE!

If you find ANY animal acting odd -- drooling, or lying on the ground without any sign of injury, keep away! Many biologists feel that bats are no more likely to carry rabies than any other mammal But just in case, don't touch or pick up grounded bats!

Myth #1   Bats Are Blind
Myth #2   Bats Fly Into Your Hair

Some people fear bats because they believe those old myths. But #1, bats can see **just fine**. And #2...well, pretend for a moment that you're a bat. Please explain **WHY** you plan to purposely get tangled up in that screeching giant's hairdo... Duh.

So, if you start to freak out when you see bats, think about the German name for the bat -- *die fledermaus* (DEE FLAY-der-mouse) -- "the flitter mouse." You're not scared of MICE, are you? Cute little mice?

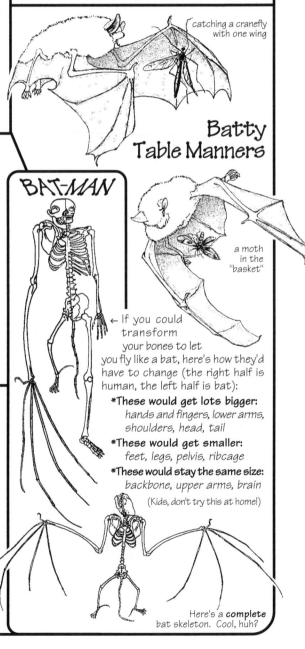

catching a cranefly with one wing

Batty Table Manners

BAT-*MAN*

a moth in the "basket"

← If you could transform your bones to let you fly like a bat, here's how they'd have to change (the right half is human, the left half is bat):

*These would get lots bigger: hands and fingers, lower arms, shoulders, head, tail

*These would get smaller: feet, legs, pelvis, ribcage

*These would stay the same size: backbone, upper arms, brain

(Kids, don't try this at home!)

Here's a **complete** bat skeleton. Cool, huh?

Chapter 35. The Yuma Myotis Bat

The piñon jays had flown away to roost in tangled shrubs along the canyon floor. The air was cool and blue by the time the Yuma myotis bat flickered into sight above the potholes.

On his way to his night roost behind a slab of red sandstone near the seep, the bat skimmed over a pool to drink, opening his mouth wide and scooping up a mouthful of water as he glided just above the surface, leaving a V-shaped ripple behind.

His evening had been spent hunting insects above

as submarines use sonar underwater. Zeroing in on the echo, he would sweep the insect into his mouth with a curled wing, or make a basket of his legs and tail and scoop it out of the air. Still flying, he would bend forward to eat out of his "basket."

The little myotis was nearly fifteen years old, and he was beginning to slow down with age. The fur on his face was sprinkled with gray hairs, and he was tired from the long evening's hunt.

He circled the pothole and swooped

the beaver pond at the mouth of the canyon. He would locate his target by squeaking out short bursts of sound too high for most ears to hear. The sound, hitting a flying insect, would bounce back to the bat as an echo, much

down over the calm and silent water for one final drink to wash down the last few furry moths he had caught near the beaver dam. Old and tired, he didn't notice the cat-sized creature crouched in the shadow of a boulder. Without a sound, it leaped high into the air and snatched him with its front paws and sharp, white teeth.

Ringtail

Bassariscus astutus (bass-uh-RISS-cuss ass-TOOT-us)
Bassar = "fox"   *iscus* = "little"   *astutus* = "cunning"

The ringtail looks a lot like a cross between a fox and a cat, but it's actually in the same family as the raccoon. It is a dainty, beautiful cat-sized omnivore, eating birds, lizards, insects, fruit and carrion. When nervous, it fluffs and curls its 17" tail above its body, trying to appear large and scary.

Ringtails live in caves and hollow trees, and may even share a den with skunks and rattlesnakes. In the 1800's they sometimes denned under miners' cabins, and since they kept the cabin areas free of mice and rats, the miners considered them odd but welcome pussycats. Being nocturnal and very secretive, they never made especially good pets.

Ringtails often hunt in pairs, or as family groups in the late summer when the cubs (three or four per litter) are learning to forage (FOR-ij -- search for food). Weighing about an ounce at birth, the young are fully grown at five months.

Caught in a Crack?   Not A Ringtail!

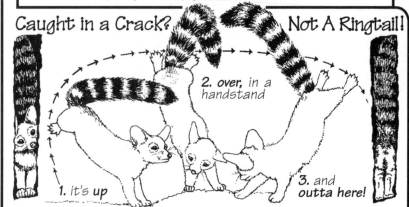

2. *over*, in a handstand

1. *it's up*

3. and *outta here!*

With a narrow body, lots of smarts, and hind feet that can swivel around to point backward, the agile (AJ-ul) ringtail can get in and out of places you wouldn't believe.

Kiss the Ringtail

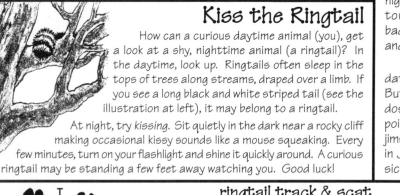

How can a curious daytime animal (you), get a look at a shy, nighttime animal (a ringtail)? In the daytime, look up. Ringtails often sleep in the tops of trees along streams, draped over a limb. If you see a long black and white striped tail (see the illustration at left), it may belong to a ringtail.

At night, try *kissing*. Sit quietly in the dark near a rocky cliff making occasional kissy sounds like a mouse squeaking. Every few minutes, turn on your flashlight and shine it quickly around. A curious ringtail may be standing a few feet away watching you. *Good luck!*

The Aztec Cacomixtle

The ringtail lives in Central America, too. Ancient Aztecs called it the rush-cat, *cacomixtle* (kak-oh-MEESH-tl) using the same "lateral L" sound they used for *coyotl* (see page 8 for a "tongue assist"). In Mexico the ringtail is called *tepemixtle*, Aztec for "bush-cat."

In the Southwest, many people call it the cacomi**s**tle, pronounced kak-oh-MISS-tull. It is also called ringtailed cat, coon cat, band-tailed cat, mountain cat, miner's cat, squirrel cat, civet cat, American civet, and raccoon fox. *Whew!*

Hummingmoth????

Thrrrrrruummmmmmm! It's dark, pitch black and something zooms by so fast it outflies the swinging beam of your flashlight. A hummingbird? No, wait -- hummingbirds don't fly at night! Wow! You've just encountered a white-lined sphinx moth, *Hyles lineata*. Found all over North America, the sphinx moth visits and pollinates flowers night and day (but mostly at dusk).

The Moon Flower

The beautiful 5-7" white trumpet-shaped flowers of the sacred datura, *Datura meteloides* (shown above), are open from dusk to dawn all summer. The flowers are pollinated by the sphinx moth and other nocturnal insects. Watch for datura at night if you go out looking for a ringtail. Don't touch the plant though -- the velvety, bad-smelling leaves can cause a nasty rash, and eating any part of the plant can kill you.

Native peoples have considered the datura to be sacred, giving them visions. But datura is a killer. Even with the "right" dose, a plant with stronger-than-average poison can be fatal. Datura is also called jimsonweed, because early American colonists in Jamestown (shortened to "Jimson") got sick from eating the leaves.

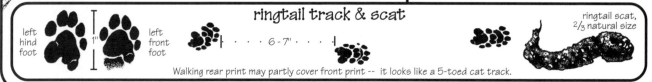

ringtail track & scat

left hind foot   1"   left front foot   6 - 7"   ringtail scat, 2/3 natural size

Walking rear print may partly cover front print -- it looks like a 5-toed cat track.

Chapter 36. The Ringtail

Snatching a bat out of midair is quite an acrobatic feat, but it was no special trick for the ringtail. Tough, strong and wiry, she was a daredevil rockclimber, searching the rimrock each night for prey. On a trip up a cliff, the little ringtail might bounce off one vertical rock face, grab an invisible clawhold on another, then enter a crack going straight up -- and bracing her hind feet on one wall and her front feet on the other, zip to the top.   No, it was an easy thing for her to catch the little myotis bat.

It was nearly dark when the ringtail finished her meal and sat grooming confidently in the deepening dusk by the little pool. The bat had been delicious, but it had been small and she was still hungry. She rose and moved like a swift shadow in the darkness -- the half moon wouldn't rise for quite awhile yet. She scrambled gracefully up a steep rock face to explore a slight noise. There she discovered and ate a rock wren which had thought itself safe in a deep crevice in the rock.

Having gone headfirst into the narrow crack, the ringtail had little room to turn around, but this was no problem. She did a handstand, walking her hind feet up the wall and down around behind, then exited head first from the crack. Most animals can't turn their feet around backward like the ringtail, and it gave her a great hunting advantage on the cliffs.

Now she needed something to take home to the youngsters at the den.   Just after moonrise, she sniffed out a dead lizard that was lodged beneath a boulder, and started home with her prize.

As she trotted along the base of a cliff, she passed near a large clump of datura with huge, white night-blooming flowers. The sweet scent of the flowers perfumed the air and the ringtail heard the whirring *"thrrrrmmmm-thrrmmmmmmm"* of a sphinx moth visiting the flowers for nectar. She paused for a moment, trying to locate the big moth -- a favorite food of ringtails -- but the moth zoomed off down the canyon, so the ringtail continued on her way.

Padding silently across soft sand, she surprised a scorpion, which scuttled out of her way -- right across the nose of a gray fox sleeping beneath a juniper tree.

Gray Fox

Urocyon cinereoargenteus (yew-ROSS-ee-on sin-EER-ee-oh-ar-JEN-tee-us)
Uro = "tail" *cyon* = "dog" *cinereus* = "ash-colored" *argenteus* = "silver"

If you see a gray fox, you may think it's a red fox, for the gray fox has rusty red fur on its sides and chest, as well as frosty gray markings. Red foxes are rufous (red-orange) with white tail tips and black legs. You *could* see a red fox in the canyons, but they're rare there, so you probably won't.

Gray foxes love trees. They like to hunt, nap and travel in trees, leaping from branch to branch on twigs as tiny as 3/4." They climb straight up the trunk like a cat, hugging it with their forelegs and pushing with their long, sharp back claws (they usually come down tail first so they can hang on better).

Four to six fuzzy black pups are born in March. They weigh about 2½ ounces each. Wrap 16 pennies in a tissue and hold it in your hand -- that's what a baby fox weighs! Full grown in 5 to 6 months, they weigh 7 to 15 *pounds* each. (A penny weighs $^1/_{100}$ of a pound. How many pennies would equal one adult fox?)

Fox Fax

When their pups are about six weeks old, gray foxes begin to bring insects, spiders, lizards and mice to the den for them to eat. By fall, the parents have taught the pups where to hunt, what to eat, and how to avoid hungry coyotes, bobcats and great horned owls.

Gray fox coloring is good camouflage in the red rocks and shadows of the canyons. Since foxes are cautious, fall is the best time to see them -- while the pups are still learning. Move quietly, look up into trees and into shadows.

gray fox

red fox

Watch for tracks. Gray foxes have larger toe pads than red foxes (fur between red fox toes almost wipes out their toe prints).

The bark of the gray fox is a harsh yap, a throat-tearing, barking scream. It's hard to imagine such a sound until you hear it.....

Skull Skills

Compare shape of the sagital (SAJ-it-ull) crests, or center areas, on the skulls of the two foxes.

See the difference?

6"

gray fox

red fox

Gray Fox Café Menu

Main Dish

With Tender Mouse
or Woodrat Appetizers

Choice Mule Deer Steak
(Aged, Dried or Rotten)
With:

Hairy Caterpillars & Crunchy Beetles
Ant, Spider & Scorpion Sprinkles
Served With Tangy Hackberry Sauce

Dessert

Prickly-pear Cactus & Manzanita Berries

Drinks

Wild Grapejuice & Juniperberry Delight

That Was No Beagle!

If you see a fox, you may get only one quick look. Study these pictures and learn the differences BEFORE you see one, so you won't muff your chance!

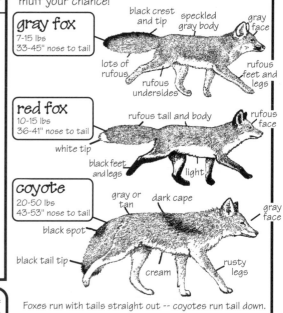

gray fox
7-15 lbs
33-45" nose to tail

black crest and tip
speckled gray body
gray face
lots of rufous
rufous undersides
rufous feet and legs

red fox
10-15 lbs
36-41" nose to tail

rufous tail and body
rufous face
white tip
black feet and legs
light

coyote
20-50 lbs
43-53" nose to tail

gray or tan
dark cape
gray face
black spot
black tail tip
cream
rusty legs

Foxes run with tails straight out -- coyotes run tail down.

Sharing the Niche

Usually, animals with similar diets and habitat needs can't share the same territory, but gray foxes and ringtails are able to live peaceably together and share their redrock canyon niche (NITCH -- habitat and food). How do they do it?

Gray foxes eat meat, fruits and berries while ringtails eat mostly meat. When one is eating lots of fruits, the other is usually eating more insects or rodents. Foxes are mostly active at dawn and dusk, while ringtails prefer the dark.

While ringtails and gray foxes may share a territory, the foxes hunt mostly on the ground in brushy areas, meadows and under trees (though they do climb), while the ringtails hunt up in trees and in the cracks and caves of steep rock faces.

They often smell each other's scent, but they seldom meet -- and that may be the very best way for such wary hunters to share their living arrangements!

gray fox track & scat

left hind foot

1 7/8"

left front foot

gray fox scat, natural size. Look for fruit seeds and insect parts.

· · 10 - 12" · · ·

A fox track looks like small dog track.

Chapter 37. The Gray Fox

The scuttling, prickly, invisible SOMETHING scratching his tender nose jerked the little fox from deep sleep with a hoarse, startled yip and a frantic leap up into the juniper tree under which he had been sleeping. The ringtail, spooked by the fleeing scorpion, the fox's yip and the scrabbling racket, leaped away up the canyon in a cascade of falling rocks -- the dead lizard still clenched in her sharp white teeth.

The breeze had carried the ringtail's scent away from the fox, and without any other clues, the fox assumed the noise of the crashing rocks had been made by his "attacker." It must be dangerous. *Huge.* He crouched in the juniper tree, quivering.

It had been a bad day -- that afternoon he'd been cornered against a cliff and harried for an hour by three bighorn ewes guarding their lambs, and he was a nervous wreck.

Several minutes went by. The fox twitched his head tensely toward each strange sound. He was too shaken and nervous to leave the tree, so he finally scratched a hollow in the shredded bark and juniper needles in the crotch of the juniper and hunkered down warily.

The half moon crept across the sky as the jittery gray fox kept watch. He saw mysterious movements in every black shadow -- there was no way to know they were just a foraging woodrat, a passing mouse, a wandering stink beetle.

"Whooo, hu-hooo, whooo-whoooo," echoed from cliff to cliff as a great horned owl called to its mate -- there was no way to know it wasn't hungry enough to grab a small gray fox. Nothing sprang from the shadows, nothing grabbed or clawed at him, and after awhile the little fox's eyelids drooped and he slept uneasily in the dense shadows under the juniper branches.

The sun, rising over the eastern rimrock at the foot of the canyon, lit up the juniper tree quite early. The fox awoke with a startled yap as several hairs were rudely yanked from his tail. Two flycatchers were fluttering overhead and the canyon echoed with the *"Pee-reer! Pee-reer!"* of their angry cries.

Ash-throated Flycatcher

Myiarchus cinerascens (my-AR-kuss sin-ur-ASS-enz)
Myia = "fly" *archos* = "one who rules" *cinerasco* = "turning to ash"

The flycatcher, whose scientific name might be translated as Lord of the Flies, does just what you'd expect -- it catches flies. And wasps, bees, bugs, cicadas, moths, grasshoppers and robberflies. It also forages for some that don't fly much, such as ants, spiders, aphids, leafhoppers and caterpillars.

In the canyon country, you will probably hear the ash-throated flycatcher before you see it. Listen for a loud, clear **"Wheet! Wheet!"** Then look for a shady perch over low shrubbery and a gray-backed, white-throated, rusty-tailed bird, smaller than a robin. darting out to catch insects with a noisy click of its bill. After catching one, it usually moves off to another perch.

When courting or feeling aggressive, the ash-throated flycatcher raises the crest of feathers on the top of its head -- perhaps to make itself look more impressive (it does).

The Hole Story

This is a cross-section of an ash-throated flycatcher nest in a tree. The lowest layer contains grass, dung and roots. Hair and fur make the nest soft.

The ash-throated flycatcher is a cavity-nester. It takes over a woodpecker nest (it may chase off the woodpeckers who are using it!) or finds a hollow branch with a knothole entrance. It will nest in a tree cavity from 3 - 20' above the ground, or on a ledge if it can't find a cavity. The nest is made with grass, matted hair (rabbit, bighorn sheep, etc.), weed stems and dried dung (animal droppings), and may also contain shed reptile skins.

Cavity nesters *usually* have pale unmarked eggs, while birds with more exposed nests *usually* have eggs that are spotted or streaked for camouflage. The streaky eggs of the ash-throated flycatcher are well camouflaged if the bird must nest on a ledge.

Here's a puzzle (but no answer): A robin nests out in the open on a branch, so why aren't its eggs streaked or spotted -- and why are they a bright, show-offy blue? Any ideas?

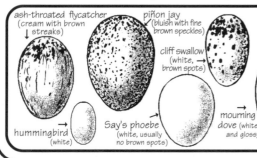

ash-throated flycatcher (cream with brown streaks)
piñon jay (bluish with fine brown speckles)
cliff swallow (white, brown spots)
raven (bluish or greenish with brown blotches)
hummingbird (white)
Say's phoebe (white, usually no brown spots)
mourning dove (white and glossy)

Chasing The Elephant

Have you ever seen birds diving, pecking and squawking at a cat? This is called *mobbing*. Sometimes five or six different kinds of birds will mob a cat, snake, dog, fox, hawk, owl, raccoon -- whatever they feel is a danger to them or their young.

When birds raise such an alarm, every other animal around knows there is danger in the neighborhood, and more birds join the mob to drive away the enemy or keep it from noticing their nest or young fledglings. Predators need to sneak up on their prey, so a noisy mob really messes up their plans. They usually leave.

You'd think small birds would fly off and hide. An ash-throated flycatcher only weighs about an ounce. A ten pound fox weighs about as much as a hundred and fifty flycatchers.

Hey, would YOU have the nerve to poke a wild animal *larger* than a very BIG elephant -- with a fork?

Egg Etiquette

If you find a nest full of eggs, **look quickly then leave** so the parents can return to keep them warm and alive. Almost all birds are protected by law, and it is illegal to collect eggs, feathers, or bird parts.

Some eggs you might see in the canyons are shown here natural size.

Chapter 38. The Ash-throated Flycatcher

The flycatchers nesting in the juniper had been awakened by the racket the night before. But when things quieted down they went back to sleep -- the female on her eggs in a cavity just above the gray fox, the male on his ledge a few yards away. They could do nothing in the dark, anyway. At dawn, the female peeked from the hole and was outraged to find the fox still napping in her tree.

Ash-throated flycatchers love a good rumpus. So instead of hiding, the flycatcher darted down and snatched a clump of tail hairs, pulling hard. *Phhht!* The fox jerked awake just as the female was joined by her mate, shrieking noisily. *"Pee-reer! Pee-reer! Chk! Chk-chk!"* they dive-bombed his ears.

The fox was crouching in the juniper crotch, ducking and snapping angrily when two ravens came flying by. Nearly two feet long, with heavy, businesslike bills, the ravens lit in the juniper with noisy *"RONK! BRONK! ARAW! RAWK!"* squawks. *"Pee-reer! ARONK! Chk-chk! KARONK! Pee-reer!"* A rock wren lit on a nearby boulder, adding its warning *"Tik-eer! Tik-eer!"* and several piñon jays arrived screaming *"QUEK! QUEK!"*

By now the noise was awesome. *"RONK! Tik-eer! ARONK! Chk-chk! QUEK! Tik-eer! BRONK! Pee-reer! BRONK! Pee-reer! ARAWK! QUEK! QUEK! BRONK! Tik-eer! RAWK!"* The canyon walls echoed and magnified the earsplitting noise. The flycatchers and the rock wren tweaked the fox's ears, back, and tail. The ravens hopped from branch to branch, coming closer. Outnumbered ten to one, the fox scrambled tail-first, down the trunk of the tree, his long, sharp claws digging deeply into the stringy bark. On the ground, he ran, the mob of birds trailing after, diving and pecking at him until he plunged to safety under a pile of boulders.

Back at the juniper tree, the flycatchers panted for a few moments, then the female slipped back to her eggs in the nest cavity. She was lucky -- they were still warm. If they had gotten cold while the nest was being defended, they wouldn't hatch. The male flycatcher flew to a lookout branch to watch for edible insects flying past and to keep an eye on the nest. If the ravens came back, they'd have to defend the nest from them -- ravens were as dangerous to eggs or nestlings as any fox!

Raven

Corvus corax (KOR-vuss KOR-aks)
Corvus = "raven" (Latin)   *corax* = "raven" (Greek)

The raven, *Corvus corax*, is found in all the northern areas of the world, and as far south as Central America. It's related to crows, jays and magpies, all of which are very smart and vocal (talkative). Its scientific name was taken from its Greek and Latin common names, which sound like raven croaks.

In the canyon country the raven usually nests on ledges or in holes in vertical cliff faces (sometimes in tall trees) in April or May. To spot a nest site, listen for loud croaking as adults approach the nest with food. The young will answer with high-pitched croaks.

Most people can't tell ravens and crows apart. Here are some clues: Both are black and large, but the raven is larger. The crow's call is a high-pitched **"KAW!"** The raven has a feathery beard. The crow's tail is flat or straight across the end, the ra**v**en's tail tip is **V**-shaped.

raven crow

Superbirds

Ravens may have the highest intelligence in the bird world, with a language of at least thirty distinct calls and "words" to communicate "*danger,*" "*someone's coming,*" "*food's here, come get it!*" "*come play*" and many other things. And when grooming and courting their mates, they hold each other's bills and croon special courting songs and sounds.

courting

Also when courting (or just goofing around) they make all kinds of show-off flights, including "barrel-rolls," hovering, and fancy tricks like flying with wingtips touching (sometimes with one bird flying upside down!) Ravens mate for life -- and since ravens live up to 20 years in the wild, they can perfect some pretty neat acrobatics. They seem to enjoy playing. What else explains

stunt flying

playing

a raven sliding again and again down a pebbly slope, or hanging by its bill from a branch, then swinging up and over in a loop-the-loop when no other bird is around to see?!

What's For Dinner?

Ravens are omnivores, and they'll eat just about any kind of meat, fresh or not. Nearly two feet long and with a wingspread of up to almost five feet, they eat rodents and young rabbits for about a third of their diet. Spiders and insects make up another third. Birds (adults, eggs and nestlings), amphibians, reptiles and carrion make up the rest.

Since ravens don't have hooked beaks or claws, they aren't able to open up a carcass to feed -- so they wait for other animals to do it. Sometimes they follow coyotes to eat their leftovers. They also dig holes with their beaks and bury or cache (KASH) food, then dig it up later to eat.

natural size

If a raven finds something so large that it can't eat the whole thing, it makes loud, yelping cries that bring ravens from miles around to share the treasure.

Ravens often hunt in the sand dunes for rodents, reptiles, bird eggs and nestlings, frogs, insects, spiders, and scorpions. Watch for their tracks there.

Bad Camp Food

Hanging around campgrounds is bad news for ravens, because people feed them unhealthy foods like candy (empty calories), white bread (little food value), and potato chips (greasy and salty), etc. Their stomachs plug up with plastic bags and foil. They may be killed by unleashed dogs or speeding vehicles.

Ravens can easily find wild food, so don't endanger them by offering snacks!

A Raven Beauty?

You couldn't honestly call raven chicks "cute." They have tiny eyes, gigantic beaks, and they're noisy.

Only a month after hatching, they've grown to almost full-size, and leave the nest to follow their parents.

Chapter 39. The Raven

Mobbing the gray fox was great sport for the ravens. But when the fox dived out of reach under the boulders, the fun was over and they flew away down the canyon to a gnarly old tree skeleton rooted in a crack on a cliff face. They lit on a twisted silver branch, and the male began to tenderly court his mate as he had courted her each spring for the past six years.

"Rur-rick-rur-ruck, kruck," the male croaked, smoothing her head feathers with his heavy bill.

"Puree-ruk, puree-ruk-pee-rick" she murmured, preening his neck contentedly with closed eyes.

The male launched himself straight up off the branch. Forty feet up, he closed his wings and dived, turning around and around in a barrel-roll, beak pointing toward the female. He braked to a stop directly in front of her with a loud *"KRAWK!"* flapping heavily. She leaped off the branch to join him in a wide circling cruise with touching wingtips. Later that day, they began carrying sticks, juniper bark, bones, strips of yucca fiber and tufts of shed bighorn sheep wool to last year's nest, a hole in the high cliff wall above the beaver pond.

When the nest was ready, the female raven laid one egg each day until six dark-spotted pale-green eggs clustered in the nest. Then she settled down in the dark hollow to brood them. The male raven would bring her food while she kept the eggs warm for the next three weeks -- crickets, carrion, lizards, grasshoppers, snakes, frogs, scorpions, mice, and one ash-throated flycatcher fledgling.

When the last chick hatched, the mother raven flew from the nest with the final eggshell and a loud *"GROKKKK."* She dropped the shell far from the nest, then flip-flopped wildly in a big arching loop through the air, croaking loudly. Her mate joined her with a *"KRONK,"* carrying a tuft of rabbit fur, and they took turns dropping and catching it. Soon they would go find food for the chicks, but just now she needed to stretch her wings!

Western Rattlesnake

Crotalus viridis (kro-TAL-uss VEER-id-us)
krot = "a rattling noise" *alus* = "making" *viridis* = "green"

Although western rattlers may be greenish-colored, the western rattlers of the redrock country usually match local rock colors. They're small, often less than 25." The midget faded rattlesnake, *Crotalus viridis concolor* (*C. v. concolor*), is mild-mannered and cream-colored with "faded" markings. On the south and east edges of the Colorado Plateau is the Hopi rattlesnake, *C. v. nuntius*, which is reddish with faint spots. The bright salmon-pink, lightly spotted Grand Canyon rattlesnake, *C. v. abyssus* lives in the Grand Canyon. Actually, you probably won't see any snakes unless you're lucky -- they hide when it's hot.

Be watchful for snakes but don't be afraid. Follow the simple rules on page 105. For many people, a bee sting is far more serious than a rattlesnake bite! Just stay alert and keep your eyes and ears open. And remember, rattlesnakes are an essential part of the ecosystem. They help keep the rodent population balanced, so don't tease or kill snakes.

Snake Art

Snakes are common in rock art. Look for zigzag or curvy lines with a head bulge at one end. In prehistoric times snakes symbolized water, which moves like a snake. One ancient group of native Americans chose the very highly respected snake for their clan symbol.

some examples...

Could YOU Be a Rattlesnake?

It is hard to really enter into the world of a rattle-snake -- for instance can you imagine:

~~~ belly-walking in concertina fashion (see page 64)
~~~ having no eyelids to close
~~~ delivering poison through *collapsible hollow fangs*
~~~ eating once a *week* or even less often
~~~ being unable to move when your body is cold

Okay, maybe you can imagine those. But what about *these*:

~~~ smelling things with your *forked tongue*
~~~ hearing with your *ribs* (vibrations)
~~~ sensing your victim *glowing in the dark*
~~~ bearing 6 to 12 live, wiggly babies at a time

Now *that's* pretty close to "outer-space-alien"!

Old Socks and Beads

When shedding, a snake's skin loosens along its lips first, sliding back over its body like a sock turning inside out. The snake rubs against rocks and sticks to scrape the old skin off. Silvery and see-through, a rattlesnake's shed skin won't have a rattle attached -- the rattles stay on the snake. Rattles don't show a snake's age -- a new button forms with each new skin, once or twice a year.

A very old snake may have up to twenty buttons in its rattle, but some usually break off. Rattles are made of the same stuff as fingernails. The loosely connected buttons clatter against each other like interlocking beads. A rattlesnake would rather warn you off than bite, so special muscles let it vibrate its tail for more than three hours without stopping. How long could you shake part of your body like that? Try it with your finger or arm.

1 week

1-2 years

old adult

adult

natural size

cut-away view of rattles

The Situlili Kachina

In the Zuni Indian culture, the rattlesnake kachina *Situlili*, dancing with a snake in its mouth, represents the spirit of fertility and life.

This ancient kachina ⟶ was carved from wood and then painted black, brown, white and red. On its head are feathers and long black hair. A real rattlesnake rattle and a turquoise bead hang from its neck on a leather thong. Tiny leather medicine pouches hang at its waist.

Hopi Indian Snake Dancers dress much this way for their ceremonial snake dances.

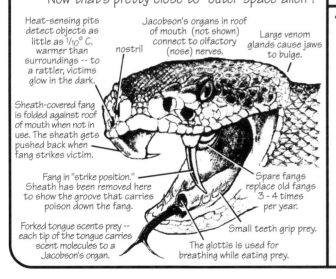

Heat-sensing pits detect objects as little as 1/10° C. warmer than surroundings -- to a rattler, victims glow in the dark.

nostril

Jacobson's organs in roof of mouth (not shown) connect to olfactory (nose) nerves.

Large venom glands cause jaws to bulge.

Sheath-covered fang is folded against roof of mouth when not in use. The sheath gets pushed back when fang strikes victim.

Fang in "strike position." Sheath has been removed here to show the groove that carries poison down the fang.

Spare fangs replace old fangs 3 - 4 times per year.

Forked tongue scents prey -- each tip of the tongue carries scent molecules to a Jacobson's organ.

Small teeth grip prey.

The glottis is used for breathing while eating prey.

Chapter 40. The Western Rattlesnake

The keen-eyed raven was hunting, watching for movement as he flew. He dipped one wing and dived steeply when he saw something slide into a horizontal crack. With a rustle of ebony feathers and a slight thump, he landed on the sand and peered into the narrow crack at the foot of the red cliff.

Deep in the crack, a rattlesnake tensed. She had felt, along her entire body, the vibration when the raven's feet hit the sand. In the little pit below each eye she could sense the heat of the raven's body against the background heat of the hot landscape. Flicking her shiny black tongue in and out, she tasted the odor of raven.

The rattlesnake squeezed deeper into the crack as the raven's beady eye appeared and stared into the darkness. The snake's rough scales whispered against the sandstone, and she nervously vibrated her tail in warning, making a sharp buzzing sound.

Although the glare from the sun blinded the raven to the dim shape of the snake, he recognized the rattling sound instantly. *Danger!* With a loud *"KRONK!"* the raven launched himself hastily into the air and resumed his hunt for food for his nestlings.

The snake slowly relaxed, but remained where she was. There was no reason to go out in the heat -- she would stay in her cool shelter until dusk.

As the afternoon heated up,
thunderclouds gathered over the mesas.
Great mountains of clouds boiled into the sky like
smoke from a forest fire.   At first the clouds' pink bellies reflected the red of the
sand and rocks below, but soon they turned gray, full of rain, sparking long snake-tongues of lightning across the sky.
Thunder rumbled all afternoon as curtains of falling rain hid the high rimrock, and light sprinkles of rain pocked the
sand in the canyon. The sharp, pungent smell of sagebrush and moist earth filled the air.

Late in the afternoon, the bighorn sheep on the high ledges began to stamp their feet and stare toward the head of the canyon. Birds fell silent, hunched tightly into their nests or against tree trunks, and alarmed ground squirrels huddled in their burrows. The rattlesnake hissed anxiously and shook her rattles. Pressed against the stone, she could feel the earth trembling, trembling. It did not stop.

Flash Flood

A flash flood can kill you "in a flash." In most parts of the U.S., a dry gully doesn't fill up with a flood of water without warning. But in the desert, when a big rain storm (called a cloudburst) occurs in the mountains or on mesa tops, there is little vegetation to soak up the water. Instead, it flows downhill, over rocks and hard earth and into gullies and canyons, where it gets funneled all together into a rushing flood of water, mud, boulders and *debris* (deh-BREE -- rubbish) moving at high speed.

When hiking in canyons, pay attention to the weather. A desert storm may be far away and barely noticeable in a canyon -- until the resulting flash flood arrives. Such storms are frequent in the summer, especially on hot afternoons when heated air flows up the canyons (hot air rises, remember?) and hits the cool, moist air higher up. This creates thunderheads, solid-looking billowing white *cumulonimbus* (KEW-mew-lo-NIM-bus) clouds that can rise higher than 30,000 feet (5½ miles). If it rains late in the afternoon, *a flash flood may not reach lower canyons until after dark.* Learn how to choose safe campsites on page 104.

Crumbling Cliffs

Why do cliffs crumble? Rain water and melting snow seep into cracks in the stone. In winter, the water freezes and swells, forcing the cracks to widen. Small cracks make shelters for canyon wildlife. But the cracks grow wider, year by year, until a chunk of cliff splits off and falls onto the jumble of rocks at the base. Over millions of years, an entire cliff will tumble down in this way. A mesa, with its rimrock and sloping sides, is just → a collapsing cliff.

psst...Your Make-up Is Smeared

The black, brown and red stains on cliffs are called *desert varnish* and they're actually large bacteria colonies. When water washes minerals down the face of a cliff, the bacteria bind with them to form thin protective coatings over themselves. Each kind of mineral *oxidizes* (rusts) and stains the cliff its own particular color.

BOOM!

How far away was that lightning flash? Remember this: Sound travels about one mile in 5 seconds.

Count like this: ⚡ "one-thousand, two-thousand, three-thousand, four-thousand, five-thousand" *RUMBLE!* Lightning was about one mile away!

This part is called the "anvil."

Forecast: SHOWERS

If you see cumulonimbus clouds like these, expect rain -- although on really hot days the rain might evaporate before it hits the ground. Watch for rainbows!

To make a typical rainbow, the sun must be less than 42° above the horizon and behind you, with the rainclouds in front of you. If you're standing on a mesa or butte (or flying in a plane) and looking down on clouds or rain, you may see a rainbow "ring" with your shadow in the center of it!

sun

this is 42°

horizon

The Canyon Treefrog *Hyla arenicolor*

You *could* call the canyon treefrog the canyon untreeunfrog because it lives on or near rocks, seldom in trees. And because it is squatty and warty, it resembles a toad more than a frog (except for its treefroggy toepads).

Its mottled skin blends with the rocks perfectly -- *if it keeps its bright yellow inner thighs out of sight.*

natural size

On a summer night, in a rocky canyon with running water and still pools, you might hear its nasal, whirring call, lasting one to three seconds. In the daytime, it's really hard to find a canyon treefrog.

Stone Jellyfish? Uh Huh!

You're hiking a canyon trail when you suddenly see, embedded in the desert sandstone, what looks like part of a ten-inch stone jellyfish or coral. Huh? Well, it may be! Many sealife fossils lie in the stone layers of the canyon country from earlier eons when it was an ocean. A flash flood can uncover amazing things.

Dinosaur tracks cross ancient mud, rippled by winds and pockmarked by an ancient rain shower -- then turned to stone. Chunks of petrified wood logs tumble down into the canyons. Indian artifacts, buried by the dust of ages are washed from ancient resting places. Flash floods destroy the current setup, but they rearrange the scenery so that new nutrients and different vegetation can take root, and new life can flourish. It's all part of the ever-changing web of life.

Who Was Here Last Night?

Stories are "written" on the sand day and night! Who was here? Search this book for their secret identities, then try your skills on **real** tracks in **real** sand or mud.
CLUE: see pages 20, 70, 76 & 96

½ natural size

Chapter 41. The Flash Flood

Suddenly, with a rumbling roar, a wall of muddy water thundered down the canyon, carrying boulders and sagebrush, bird nests, and all kinds of other things along with it. Ground squirrels and mice tried frantically to outrun the water. Warblers, piñon jays and wrens rose into the air and fluttered above their nests in panic. Woodrats, whose nests were mostly above the waterline of the flash flood, darted deep into their nests or rock crevices and huddled together quivering. The floodwaters carried an immense amount of woody trash, leaving tangles of sagebrush, grass, yucca and juniper fibers trailing from tree branches high above the canyon floor.

The flood overflowed the potholes near the seep, and then, barely half an hour after it had begun, it was past, slowed to a trickle, leaving behind pools and puddles, rippled hills of mud, soaked sand and tumbled boulders. Tangled heaps of gnarly juniper, pine and oak branches were piled up against everything that hadn't been washed away.

The flash flood was a disaster for some animals. Birds with low nests lost their eggs or young, although many of them would rebuild and nest again. Some animals hiding in burrows or holes were drowned. Others were swept away by the water.

But other animals lucked out. Ravens and vultures stuffed their chicks with flood victims. Coyotes carried drowned rabbits, lizards and snakes home to their pups. All predators -- owls, hawks, ringtails, foxes and others -- ate well, for homeless creatures, with nests and burrows swept away or filled with mud or sand, were easier to catch than those with a familiar hole to hide in.

Adult spadefoot toads dug up to the surface through the wet sand and hopped vigorously across the sandstone terrace to court and mate in the brimming potholes. A canyon treefrog, perched high on a rock, blinked and stretched, showing its bright yellow inner legs. It dropped to the soaked sand and hopped to the edge of a pothole. Diving down into the muddy water, it came nose to nose with another male canyon treefrog which had survived the flood in its hiding place under a rock. Later that night, as rain dimpled the water's surface, their hollow, nasal calls rose into the star-studded night.

"a-a-a-a-a-a......a-a-a-a-a-a....." they cried, calling the female treefrogs to come mate with them in the pool.

"Waa-waa-waa-waa-waa" sang the male spadefoot toads to their females.

And the length of the canyon throbbed with the "Waa-Waa.... a-a-a-a-a-a..... Waa-Waa.... a-a-a-a-a-a..... Waa-Waa.... a-a-a-a-a-a..... Waa-Waa.... a-a-a-a-a-a.....Waa-Waa...." of life in the wake of disaster.

Desert Cottontail

Sylvilagus auduboni (sill-vih-LAY-guss aw-doo-BON-ee)
sylvi = "woods" *lagos* = "hare" *auduboni* = "named for Audubon"

The desert cottontail rabbit looks much like an ordinary cottontail, although it may be lighter in color as many desert animals are, and its ears are a little bigger to help it cool off. Be sure to read about the black-tailed jackrabbit on page 14 to find out how big ears help hares and rabbits cool down.

Look for the desert cottontail in open areas -- valleys, low hills, and at the mouths of canyons. It spends its time among sagebrush, blackbrush and rabbitbrush, in the vicinity of piñon and juniper trees.

The cottontail is active at dawn or dusk, but on cool or cloudy days you may see one anytime. When it's hot, it tries to keep out of the sunshine. The desert cottontail seldom rests in shallow depressions dug under shrubs as other cottontails do -- instead, it may slip into a brush pile or a badger hole for a nap or even climb a sloping tree to pick up a cool breeze. (So we should look in trees for desert cottontails? Hmmmm.)

Bare Baby Bunny

Born in a burrow underground, a baby cottontail is hairless and helpless at first. But it grows quickly -- its eyes open at 10 days, and in two weeks it's out of the nest. It can breed at 3½ months, and may have its own litter of two or three nestlings by the end of its **first summer!**

newborn
cottontail
2/3 natural size

Jackrabbit vs. Cottontail

sutures

A skull contains many bones. The places where the bones join are called sutures (SOO-churz). Young animals have simple, shallow sutures, but an older animal's sutures are deeply interlaced

Sutures strengthen a skull. For instance, sutures on a buck deer's skull are extremely deep and interlocking to reinforce the skull and absorb the shock of clashing, crashing antlers in autumn.

and
sutures
old animal   young animal

For many Native American tribes, the great horned owl is an important symbol. It represents thunderclouds, which bring life-giving rain to the desert. It stands for death or the underworld because it flies during darkness. In Navajo tradition, an owl is a bad omen.

But in Hopi tradition, it brings summer heat for growing corn and beans. Hopis know owls kill rodents that would eat their food crops.

The Horned Owl Kachina represents fertility in Hopi ceremonies. Maybe owls held a similar place in Ancestral Puebloan ceremonies.

Blackbrush
Coleogyne ramosissima

Need a safe place to hang out? Try underneath a blackbrush -- if you can get there in one piece! A member of the rose family, the blackbrush has stickery thorns, small gray-green leaves and tiny yellow flowers. The leaves are a favorite food of mule deer and bighorn sheep.

The blackbrush is a "safe house" for small creatures like rabbits and mice -- the thorns may slow down their pursuers long enough for them to escape out the far side.

Carryin' Carrion Home

Some predators, such as owls and snakes, are programmed to take only live prey. If it isn't warm and moving, they won't touch it. Predators that **will** eat carrion (long-dead meat) have a real advantage during floods or fires. For awhile, at least, their food doesn't run away or fight back, and if they survive the disaster that killed dinner, they'll eat very well for awhile.

Vultures eat **only** carrion. But the gray fox, ringtail, grasshopper mouse, bobcat, raven, coyote, chipmunk and other animals eat carrion if they come across it while they are hunting.

(Do people eat carrion? What about "aged" meat?)

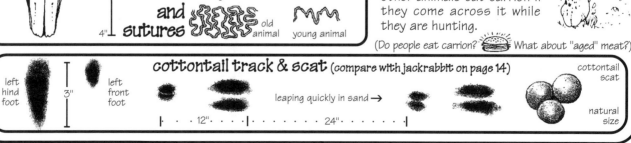

cottontail track & scat (compare with jackrabbit on page 14)

left hind foot   3"   left front foot   leaping quickly in sand →   cottontail scat   natural size

|· · · 12" · · ·|· · · · 24" · · · · · ·|

Chapter 42. The Desert Cottontail

The half-grown desert cottontail was picking his way between broken slabs of fossilized sand dunes when he felt the ground begin to tremble. At a faint low grumble of sound from up the canyon, both ears twitched forward intently and he rose up on his hind legs beneath a holly-leafed Fremont barberry shrub to get a better look. He could see nothing unusual, but a rolling gust of cool air from upcanyon, smelling of crushed greens and wet soil, made him suddenly uneasy. He dropped down to huddle nervously under a nearby blackbrush, for a cottontail's first reaction to danger is to scrunch down and try to become invisible. But that's no way to escape a flood.

Within seconds, the surging wall of muddy, boulder-filled churning water found his hiding place and it was too late to run. The cottontail was tumbled head over heels into the water, where he was raked by branches, swirled in gritty rapids, and slammed against rocks. A big wave flung him out onto a muddy bank.

He lay dazed and half drowned, barely alive. The flood waters, brown as chocolate milk and full of rubbish and rolling, crashing boulders, finally began to dwindle. The rumble sank to a mutter, then a slow gurgling trickle, then the *"plink, plunk, plink"* of water dripping off rocks into pools.

In time, the soaked and battered cottontail might have been able to drag himself under a bush to hide and regain his strength. But predators were patrolling the canyon, and the rabbit was in plain sight on the mud, one leg jerking feebly every few seconds.

Red-tailed hawks don't eat carrion. If the rabbit hadn't moved, the cruising redtail would have ignored him. But when she saw his leg twitch, she instantly dived. The big, yellow talons clenched tightly around the furry chest, and the rabbit was dead in seconds. Beating her wings heavily, the redtail rose into the air with her prize.

Red-tailed Hawk

Buteo jamaicensis (BEW-tee-oh juh-may-ih-SEN-sus)
Buteo = "falcon or hawk"   *jamaicensis* = "belonging to Jamaica"

Also called the redtail, hen hawk and red hawk, the red-tailed hawk is the most common hawk in the U.S., and the one you're likely to see in the canyon country. Redtail markings are extremely variable -- even expert bird watchers sometimes have trouble identifying redtails. But if a hawk you're watching turns in flight and flashes a cinnamon-red tail, *that's a redtail.* Unfortunately, a young red-tailed hawk *isn't* red-tailed. Its tail is brown with six to ten narrow black bars. Oh, well....

The red-tailed hawk is found from the interior of Alaska to Panama. It is big, with a wingspread of 45" to 58" -- that's almost *five feet!* It isn't a picky eater. It will eat just about anything that wiggles, from earthworms to crows to catfish to skunks to turtles to snakes to grasshoppers and crickets, etc. That's probably one reason it is so widespread -- it takes advantage of almost every kind of live food available.

After eating, it upchucks a pellet of parts it can't digest.

The Growing Machine

A redtail egg is 2¼" long. It is white with reddish-brown blotches and speckles. The fuzzy white chick grows with incredible speed. At three weeks its wing feathers are about 4½" long and are bursting out of their pinfeather sheaths. At seven weeks, before it can fly really well, it leaves the nest.

just hatched

3 weeks old, about 1/3 natural size

Mantling

When a hawk eats prey on the ground, it often stands over it and *mantles,* holding its wings up in a protective curtain around its prey for awhile, to tell others to keep away. It may continue to mantle while it eats if it feels uneasy. Mantle is another word for cape (like Superman's) and it does look like it's spreading its cape over its dinner.

A young red-tailed hawk mantles. Young birds have barred tails.

Mousetraps

Try to avoid "coming to grips" with raptors like eagles or redtails. With their incredible talons (TAL-uns -- claws) they'll win "hands down" every time!

²/5 natural size (Owwwwwwwch!)

Aerial Courtship

Redtail courtship is a noisy affair. The hawks circle and soar high in the air screaming like someone in terrible pain:

"kreee-e-e-e-e" "kreee-e-e-e-e-ahhhh"

They mate on the wing, too. The male circles high above the soaring female then dives. She turns on her back in midair and reaches toward him with her talons. He spreads his wings and tail feathers to slow his dive, and when they meet, they mate -- quickly.

It's a Hawk (I think)

Identifying the big flying birds can be frustrating. In the canyon country, a large soaring bird might be an eagle, hawk, raven, falcon or vulture. The silhouettes below show some of the differences (see also page 16). The main differences are shown below, but you can find more complete help in a bird guide -- guides with paintings show details and color best.

raven -- look for the V-shaped tail tip.

eagle -- shaped like a hawk but much larger

hawk -- smaller than an eagle

falcon -- look for narrow, pointed wings

vulture -- a small, bald head and a long tail

Here are the hawks you're most likely to see in the canyons.

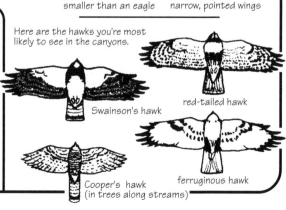

Swainson's hawk

red-tailed hawk

Cooper's hawk (in trees along streams)

ferruginous hawk

Chapter 43. The Red-tailed Hawk

The cottontail was just what the red-tailed hawk needed, for she was being chased by her two hungry, screaming fledglings. She rose high above them and dropped the rabbit. The fastest chick snagged the cottontail in midair just before it hit the mesa, then crash-landed with a thump. Still holding on, the fledgling screamed and arched her wings over the rabbit as her littermate landed nearby. The threat was clear, even without words: "BACK OFF, BROTHER!" The second chick peered enviously at the rabbit, his stomach growling. But more food was on the way -- the other redtail parent flew into sight with a half-drowned rattlesnake clutched in his talons. The hungry chick faced into the breeze and leaped into the air flapping his wings vigorously.

The adult landed in the branches of an old dead pine that was anchored just below the mesa top. Coasting down to land on a branch beneath the adult, the young redtail eyed the struggling rattlesnake anxiously. He reached out and pecked at it then dodged quickly behind the tree trunk as the snake whipped back and forth. Gathering courage, the chick reached out with his talons and grabbed the snake tightly. Stretched between the two birds, the snake couldn't move, and the chick killed it with a flurry of pecks to its head. Only then did the adult redtail drop his end of the snake. The chick tore it apart and ate greedily until nothing was left -- not even the rattle.

The adult red-tailed hawks were very tired. The fledglings still could not fly or hunt well enough to feed themselves yet, and depended on their parents for everything. Since the adults also needed to eat enough prey to keep themselves strong, they were forced to hunt every daylight hour. Easily-caught flood victims helped a lot, but it was often a long time between meals. The "teenaged" chicks seemed to think they were starving.

Sometimes a hawk fledgling, screeching hungrily from a sagebrush or following its parents for a handout, would spot a lizard and dive down to pounce on it. Lively lizards could usually escape, but the chase was good training even if the lizard got away.

Side-blotched Lizard

Uta stansburiana (YEW-tuh   stanz-burr-ee-AY-nuh)
Uta = "named for Ute Indians"   *stansburiana* = "named for Stansbury"

There are several varieties of side-blotched lizards. The one most commonly found in the redrock country is *Uta s. uniformis*. It is light brown with dark markings and it may have tiny white or sometimes sparkling turquoise-blue spots. The blotch in the armpit is very obvious. This is the little lizard (4 to 6½ inches, including the tail) you're most likely to see, even on cold, cloudy days when other lizards stay squeezed into their crevices.

It's a very lively fly catcher. It creeps around searching for winged insects, then leaps quickly and snatches them before they can take flight. That takes *speed!* If a side-blotched lizard feels threatened, it may slip behind a rock or disappear into a crack or hole, which it may have dug itself. Digging a burrow is unusual for a lizard, but side-blotched lizards do it.

This lizard likes company -- other side-blotched lizards, anyway -- and they're often seen in pairs or family groups. Females lay three *clutches* (sets) of two to six eggs each summer.

Who Needs a Black Armpit?

The "side-blotch" of the side-blotched lizard is found in its armpit. It may be black or dark blue. We aren't sure why dark blotches would be useful markings to have (maybe it flashes them to startle an attacker?), but whatever the reason, they sure make identification easier!

Lizard tracks show tail drag marks.

natural size

Mormon Tea (*Ephedra viridis*)

This shrub is related to piñons and junipers, having pretty yellow flower-like cones instead of flowers (see p. 69, far left). Also called joint-fir, it is leafless, so it photosynthesizes (FO-toh-SIN-thuh-sy-zez -- creates food) within its jointed, green stems.

It contains *ephedrine* (eh-FED-rin), found in nasal decongestants. Native Americans brew tea and a lovely tan dye from its stems. Early Mormons used it as a coffee substitute, but recent studies have found it might have some harmful effects-- don't try it!

Jerusalem Cricket

The Jerusalem cricket, *Stenopelmatus fuscus*, looks like a cricket that pumps iron. It's big, muscular, shiny and deeply tanned -- a real beach dude. A lot of people think it's poisonous or at least vicious, but it's not -- although it *will* nip if handled roughly (wouldn't you?). Its Spanish name is *niña de la tierra* or Child of the Earth, and Navajo Indians call it woh-seh-tsinni, Bald Old Man. It's active at night and eats insects, plant roots and decayed plants.

natural size

Watch for its tracks in sand.

saguaro (suh-WAR-oh) cactus

Stick 'em Up!

Cacti (KAK-tye -- one is a cact*us*, two are cact*i*) come in a lot of shapes and sizes. When most people think of "a cactus" they have something like this in mind. But the cacti in the redrock country tend to look more like this: or this:

prickly pear
Opuntia (oh-PUN-tee--uh)

fishhook cactus
Sclerocactus (SKLAIR-oh-cactus)

Whatever the shape, don't get too close to any of them. They evolved the spines to avoid being eaten. The prickly pear cactus has big spines PLUS nearly invisible little spines (called glochids -- GLAW-kids) that are almost impossible to remove. The fishhook cactus can give you a lot of pain, too.

Check out the *Opuntia* for lice -- *plant* lice, that is -- called cochineal (ko-shin-EEL) bugs! Don't worry -- plant lice don't crawl around on people and they won't bite you! Look for clumps of white fuzz on a prickly pear pad (leaf) or fruit. These are the cottony wax coverings of tiny bright-red insects that were once used to make dye. The British used cochineal dye to color their red jackets -- remember Paul Revere's famous cry "The Redcoats are coming!"

Indian Paintbrush

Many kinds of desert plants have been used as natural dyes. The lovely Indian paintbrush, *Castilleja* (cas-tih-LAY-uh), makes a deep brown dye for Navajo rugs.

The "flower" parts of the paintbrush aren't petals, they're bracts. Plant bracts are usually green, but Indian paintbrush bracts are orange, yellow, scarlet or lavender, and they greatly brighten desert landscapes.

Who Made That Little Hole?

In the canyon country one can't help noticing the little holes in the ground. They're all over the place, all shapes and sizes. Don't you wonder what made them and what might be inside? Here are some clues and the very best advice: *keep your hands and fingers out of them -- because who **knows** what's inside them **NOW?***

lizard   millipede   scorpion   spider   anthill   wasp

Chapter 44. The Side-blotched Lizard

The young red-tailed hawk was flying to the night roost just before dusk when he saw movement in the sand dunes at the foot of the canyon -- a big, tan Jerusalem cricket was plodding across the sand, a perfect target for a hungry hawk chick. He couldn't miss! The hawk dropped like a rock, wings folded and talons reaching. But a frisky puff of breeze swung him sideways, and dropped him in a shrubby patch of Mormon tea and Indian paintbrush with a great crackle of breaking twigs. He scrambled out grumpily with feathers ruffled and out of place, glaring at the cricket. The young hawk's clumsy landing had given the cricket plenty of time to squeeze safely under the sharp spines of a nearby barrel cactus. The hawk probed under the cactus, trying to rake it out, but the cactus spines stabbed the tender skin between his toe scales and he jerked his foot back out with a shriek.

He was about to launch into the air again when his keen eyes spotted a lizard dragging itself through the dunes a short distance away. A little side-blotched lizard, half stunned by a flying branch during the hawk's crash-landing, was feebly trying to creep away. With a triumphant squawk, the hawk dashed across the sand in three great, flopping leaps, and grabbed the lizard. He crouched, peering around, daring anyone to steal his prize. There was no one in sight. He ripped the lizard in half with his hooked beak, gulping hungrily. Forget the cricket -- this was his best catch so far!

When he had finished, he groomed his scrambled feathers back into place, then peered around. Now what? Hawks don't like to fly after dark and the night roost was far away. The old cottonwood tree by the beaver pond looked like a fair sleeping spot, so the young hawk flew through the dim evening light to a high branch near the trunk to spend his first night all alone.

Mourning Dove

Zenaida macroura (zen-AY-duh   muh-KROO-ruh)
Zenaida = "for Princess Zénaida" *makros* = "long" *oura* = "tail"

Many people think the **"coo"** of the mourning dove is one of the loveliest of our native bird songs. It does sound a bit sad, which is why it's called a *mourning* dove. But in reality, a cooing dove is courting, marking its property boundaries or warning away intruders, not crying over some sad memory.

The mourning dove is found throughout the U.S. and ranges from Alaska to Mexico. It is hunted as a game bird in many states, although it is too small to make much of a meal. The male is a bit larger than the female, and if you see them together you can tell them apart because the female is slimmer and, well, more *feminine* looking, while the male looks more muscular and *masculine*. Both have long, tapering tails with white edges. They mate for life. Northern birds migrate south in the winter.

You might hear them before you see them, because in addition to their cooing they have musical flight. Their wings clap and make a very distinctive wavering whistle as they fly.

You say "pigeon," I say "dove!"

So, which is right? Both. A pigeon is a dove is a pigeon. Rock dove is the real name for city pigeons. Wild rock doves nest in cliffs in Europe, but skyscrapers suit our rock dove "pigeons" just fine. If we call rock doves "pigeons," should we call the "white dove of peace" a "pigeon" since it's just a white rock dove? But "peace pigeon" doesn't sound nearly as pretty as "peace dove!"

Feeding the Squabs

A pigeon or dove chick is called a squab -- that's an old Scandinavian word for "soft and fat." Scandinavians raised squabs for the dinner table, so "squab" probably described a ready-to-eat chick.

Seeds are not terrific food for baby birds. So a dove eats and digests seeds in the normal way, but in its crop, where other birds store food while eating, it produces "pigeon milk" which is very rich in fat, proteins and vitamins. It's much like rabbit milk, except that it's thick like cottage cheese.

Dove Talk

Want to talk to doves? Join your hands together to form a large, airtight cavity. Hook your thumbs over your nearest index finger, then part your thumbs about 1/8" (see the illustrations). Put wet lips over your thumb knuckles, and blow down past the opening. Experiment with hole size and shape, the volume and the angle of your breath, and make sure there are no leaks. Once you're cooing, try a mourning dove call. It should sound like this:

"kooo-ooo-$_{ahl}$ koooooo$_o$ kooo kooo"

Make it last about four seconds. It sounds exactly like a mourning dove. Or you can talk to them by copying their call with your voice. They may answer.

blow air down past your thumbs

To coo a higher note, lift your index finger.

High Style in Dovesville

The mourning dove dresses in stylish pinkish-lavenders, grays, and soft browns. Black spots accent plush wing covers and tail, and flirty black beauty spots decorate each cheek. Catching the light, neck feathers flash a showy pink to match the rosy feet. Powder-blue eye shadow sweetly outlines sparkling black eyes. Tail feathers are glamour-tipped with white. High fashion for all seasons.

chick pecks at red area here

The hungry squab pecks a soft red area at the base of the dove's bill. The dove opens its mouth so the squab can poke in its bill and suck up the "milk" which the dove pumps up from its crop. The sucking noise can be heard from several feet away. Actually, only the female does this at first, but after the male sees her feeding the squabs for a few days he begins to produce milk too -- and just in time, as the squabs get bigger and hungrier.

At five days, the doves start to include seeds, insects, spiders and worms with the milk, and by the time the squabs leave the nest at fourteen days the mix is only 5% milk. Doves may produce two or three broods of nestlings per summer.

Apache Jumping Spider

Jumping spiders cruise plants for prey, and can spot it from several inches away with their HUGE eyes!

The Apache jumping spider (1/2" long) has a bright velvety orange abdomen.

Air Conditioning

Doves don't remove chick poop from the nests like other birds do, so it's a good thing their loose, airy nests give things a chance to dry out!

Chapter 45. The Mourning Dove

Redtail hawks are late risers, roosting until the day warms and air currents start to rise. This makes it easier for them to soar and search for food. So the young redtail was still fluffed up in sleep when the mourning doves awoke. The male dove was courting the female, but she hadn't yet accepted him. They had spent an uneasy night in the cottonwood tree, for the hawk had come to roost after sunset, and they'd been afraid to fly away into the dark.

Now, the sun rose over the eastern rimrock and warmed the upper branches of the cottonwood. The doves crouched on their branch in alarm as the hungry young redtail stretched his wings, legs and tail. To their great relief, he groomed his feathers for only a moment, then flew off to find his parents. He needed help to fill the empty spot in his belly !

In the crisp morning air, scented with sage-brush, cottonwood and rich odors from the beaver marsh, the male dove resumed his courting. He flew off the branch with loudly clapping wings, then rose more than a hundred feet into the air. There he folded his wings like a hawk and spiraled down toward his lady, braking with his tail spread in a beautiful fan. He landed beside her, puffed out his chest and bowed until his beak nearly touched her pink feet. Then he rose, bobbing his tail, and cried *"kooo-ooo-ah! koooooo koooo koooo!"*

She looked away, ignoring him, and flew to the ground to look for grass seeds. He repeated his dive-bow-coo display again and again. By afternoon, she began to be interested, and by evening they had mated. Later that week, with much cooing and bill-holding, they began to build the nest, the male delivering twigs for the female to poke into place.

Their finished nest, fifteen feet up the tree, was a flimsy platform of twigs. The two pale eggs were visible from beneath, for mourning doves don't build sturdy nests. The male incubated the eggs each day from about nine to five, and the female took the longer night shift -- typical mourning dove behavior. When the chicks hatched, each adult spent hours each day away from the nest, eating seeds, spiders and insects in order to make plentiful "pigeon milk" for the chicks.

Cottonwood Tree

Populus sp. (POP-yew-lus SPEE-sheez)
Popul = "many moving leaves"   sp. = "some species"

The Romans knew the poplar tree, and they named it with their word for people (*popul*) perhaps because its numerous leaves were continuously in motion like crowds of people.

Cottonwood trees are poplars, rising huge and ancient along desert waterways. Towering fifty to ninety feet and as much as three feet in diameter, they provide welcome shade and homes for birds and animals that prefer to nest or den in big trees. Limbs and trunks rot out, making roomy cavities, and many insects find food and shelter in and under the deeply cracked bark and among the leaves. In spring, the white cottony fuzz of the mature seeds (from female trees only) gives cottonwoods their name.

At lower elevations, you'd find Fremont (*P. fremontii*) and plains cottonwoods (*P. sargentii*). Higher up are the lanceleaf (*P. acuminata*) and narrowleaf cottonwoods (*P. angustifolia*). Poplars are members of the willow family, and young narrowleaf poplars are often mistaken for willows.

Putting The Squeeze On

Most people are surprised to discover that the gopher snake, *Pituophis melanoleucus* (also called bullsnake), is like a miniature boa constrictor. You've heard scary stories about giant boas squeezing humans to a pulp then swallowing them. If a gopher snake were bigger, it could cause nightmares. But it averages only four feet, so no fear!

If you hear birds mobbing something near the ground, it may be a gopher snake preparing its meal (squeezing, actually). The gopher snake is a natural and necessary part of the environment, designed for eating rodents and birds. Once it has its loops around dinner, you can't rescue the victim -- so don't even try.

When they're not eating, gopher snakes are calm and pleasant. Unfortunately, they look a lot like rattlesnakes, so they are often killed by mistake. Note: if it's constricting (squeezing something), it's not a rattler. (See also pages 64 and 82.)

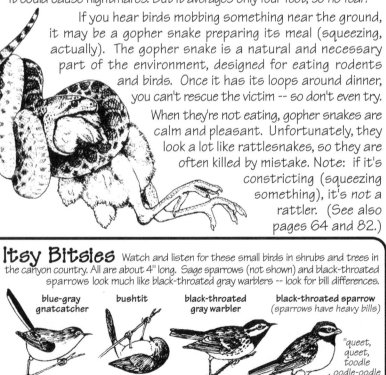

Itsy Bitsies
Watch and listen for these small birds in shrubs and trees in the canyon country. All are about 4" long. Sage sparrows (not shown) and black-throated sparrows look much like black-throated gray warblers -- look for bill differences.

blue-gray gnatcatcher
"tseee"

bushtit
"tsit, tsit, tsit, tsit"

black-throated gray warbler
"swee, swee, perswee, sik"

black-throated sparrow
(sparrows have heavy bills)
"queet, queet, toodle oodle-oodle oodle"

At The Cottonwood Shop

Besides making wonderful nesting and den sites for wildlife, cottonwood trees are useful in many other ways. Just *seeing* one is useful -- cottonwood trees say "water is here!" and in a desert, that can save your life, even if you have to dig for the water.

Cottonwood seeds are surrounded by a cottony halo of fluff which takes the seed for a ride on a breeze. If a cottonwood seed drops into a damp area, a seedling will soon sprout.

Broken-off cottonwood branches or twigs often put out roots and grow if they get partly buried in moist sand or dirt.

The fuzzy fluff sometimes collects in drifts that look like snow. The soft fibers make good nesting material for birds like gnatcatchers, hummingbirds, phoebes and goldfinches.

The inner bark, buds, catkins, leaves, and twigs of the cottonwood are all wildlife food. American Indian canyon dwellers harvested tender cottonwood buds to eat in spring. Cottonwood and willow leaves and buds contain salicylic acid, the main ingredient in aspirin.

A Tree For All Reasons

Various American Indian tribes hollow out cottonwood logs to make ceremonial drums. Kachinas can be carved from cottonwood roots. Young shoots are used like willows for weaving baskets. Ancestral Puebloans made cottonwood platters (see page 98).

Scuttle your Zapper!

Most people who own bug zappers (you know, those little electric cages that electrocute bugs in a blue flash) buy them to wipe out mosquitoes. Some campers even plug them into their generators in campgrounds to keep their site bug-free. Recent research done by Douglass Tallamy at the University of Delaware on six zappers placed within two miles of water (streams and marshes) discovered that out of 13,789 zapped insects in one summer only 31 were female mosquitoes (males don't bite) or biting flies. The rest of the victims were aquatic insects that would have made fine food for fish, and flying insects that could have been eaten by bats and small fly-catching birds.

Mosquitoes aren't attracted to the ultraviolet trap! UNPLUG THAT THING!

Chapter 46. The Cottonwood Tree

One morning, disaster struck. The day was hot and the adult doves had flown up the canyon to forage, leaving their chicks alone in the nest. Suddenly, a pair of blue-gray gnatcatchers which had been weaving cottonwood fluff into their nest on a nearby branch started to shriek alarm calls.

A hungry gopher snake was rippling up the cottonwood tree. Reaching the dove nest, the snake peered in at the nine-day-old squabs, almost as large as robins. He flicked his black tongue in and out to pick up their scent. The gnatcatchers darted and pecked frantically at the intruder to drive him away, but he ignored them.

The mourning dove squabs huddled together in panic as the gopher snake oozed in beside them. He whipped several coils of his body around a struggling nestling and began to squeeze. A shower of twigs fell from the flimsy nest and it tipped to one side, dumping the snake and his victim over the edge where they slithered down the trunk of the tree to the ground. The snake kept right on squeezing. When the nestling stopped moving, the snake opened his mouth wide, unhinging his lower jaws from his upper skull. Now he could enlarge his mouth enough to get it around the chick. He began to work his teeth over the squab's head. Soon the nestling, which was nearly three times the width of the snake, was just a bulge halfway down his body. Opening his mouth wide again, the snake wiggled his lower jaw from side to side until it slipped back into place, then he slid slowly away to find a quiet burrow to curl up in while he digested his food.

High in the cottonwood tree, the remaining squab huddled in the trashed nest. The nest was damaged, but it would hold together a few more days until the squab was able to fly.

The upset gnatcatchers began to tear their own nest apart, as gnatcatchers often do when a site they have chosen turns out to be unsafe. They started building another nest higher up in the cottonwood tree with scraps from the old nest.

They gathered new nest materials, too, foraging in the willows and rabbitbrush for small spiders and insects and the tasty caterpillars of sagebrush checkerspot butterflies.

The adult mourning doves, unaware that their family was now smaller, quietly fed on Indian rice grass seeds in the warm sunlight further up the canyon.

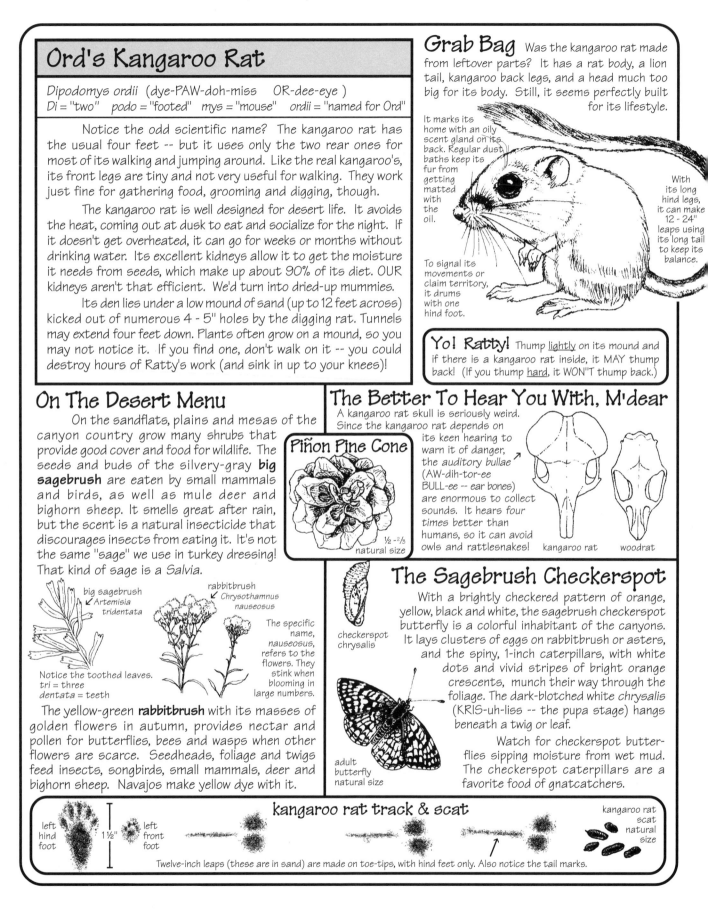

Ord's Kangaroo Rat

Dipodomys ordii (dye-PAW-doh-miss   OR-dee-eye)
Di = "two"   *podo* = "footed"   *mys* = "mouse"   *ordii* = "named for Ord"

Notice the odd scientific name? The kangaroo rat has the usual four feet -- but it uses only the two rear ones for most of its walking and jumping around. Like the real kangaroo's, its front legs are tiny and not very useful for walking. They work just fine for gathering food, grooming and digging, though.

The kangaroo rat is well designed for desert life. It avoids the heat, coming out at dusk to eat and socialize for the night. If it doesn't get overheated, it can go for weeks or months without drinking water. Its excellent kidneys allow it to get the moisture it needs from seeds, which make up about 90% of its diet. OUR kidneys aren't that efficient. We'd turn into dried-up mummies.

Its den lies under a low mound of sand (up to 12 feet across) kicked out of numerous 4 - 5" holes by the digging rat. Tunnels may extend four feet down. Plants often grow on a mound, so you may not notice it. If you find one, don't walk on it -- you could destroy hours of Ratty's work (and sink in up to your knees!)

Grab Bag

Was the kangaroo rat made from leftover parts? It has a rat body, a lion tail, kangaroo back legs, and a head much too big for its body. Still, it seems perfectly built for its lifestyle.

It marks its home with an oily scent gland on its back. Regular dust baths keep its fur from getting matted with the oil.

With its long hind legs, it can make 12 - 24" leaps using its long tail to keep its balance.

To signal its movements or claim territory, it drums with one hind foot.

Yo! Ratty!

Thump <u>lightly</u> on its mound and if there is a kangaroo rat inside, it MAY thump back! (If you thump <u>hard</u>, it WON"T thump back.)

On The Desert Menu

On the sandflats, plains and mesas of the canyon country grow many shrubs that provide good cover and food for wildlife. The seeds and buds of the silvery-gray **big sagebrush** are eaten by small mammals and birds, as well as mule deer and bighorn sheep. It smells great after rain, but the scent is a natural insecticide that discourages insects from eating it. It's not the same "sage" we use in turkey dressing! That kind of sage is a *Salvia*.

big sagebrush
↙ *Artemisia tridentata*

Notice the toothed leaves.
tri = three
dentata = teeth

rabbitbrush
↙ *Chrysothamnus nauseosus*

The specific name, *nauseosus*, refers to the flowers. They stink when blooming in large numbers.

The yellow-green **rabbitbrush** with its masses of golden flowers in autumn, provides nectar and pollen for butterflies, bees and wasps when other flowers are scarce. Seedheads, foliage and twigs feed insects, songbirds, small mammals, deer and bighorn sheep. Navajos make yellow dye with it.

Piñon Pine Cone

½ -²⁄₃ natural size

The Better To Hear You With, M'dear

A kangaroo rat skull is seriously weird. Since the kangaroo rat depends on its keen hearing to warn it of danger, the auditory bullae (AW-dih-tor-ee BULL-ee -- ear bones) are enormous to collect sounds. It hears four times better than humans, so it can avoid owls and rattlesnakes!

kangaroo rat   woodrat

The Sagebrush Checkerspot

checkerspot chrysalis

With a brightly checkered pattern of orange, yellow, black and white, the sagebrush checkerspot butterfly is a colorful inhabitant of the canyons. It lays clusters of eggs on rabbitbrush or asters, and the spiny, 1-inch caterpillars, with white dots and vivid stripes of bright orange crescents, munch their way through the foliage. The dark-blotched white chrysalis (KRIS-uh-liss -- the pupa stage) hangs beneath a twig or leaf.

Watch for checkerspot butterflies sipping moisture from wet mud. The checkerspot caterpillars are a favorite food of gnatcatchers.

adult butterfly natural size

kangaroo rat track & scat

left hind foot   1½"   left front foot

kangaroo rat scat natural size

Twelve-inch leaps (these are in sand) are made on toe-tips, with hind feet only. Also notice the tail marks.

Chapter 47. The Ord's Kangaroo Rat

The kangaroo rat was asleep when the gopher snake started his long slither into her burrow for a nap. The rat's burrow was a maze of crisscrossing tunnels at various levels, and the rat was napping on the level just below where the snake stopped to sleep off his squab dinner.

The slight vibrations made by the snake's movements just over her head woke the rat. She thumped anxiously with one hind foot, then crept up the tunnel to try to locate the intruder in the inky blackness. Rounding a corner, the rat sensed the gopher snake ahead. She quickly turned away from him and dug furiously with her front paws. Then, using her tail as a prop, she thrust her big hind feet forward, hooked her toes over the loosened soil, and kicked backward powerfully, showering the pile of sandy earth onto the snake. The snake hissed and coiled back as far as he could in the tight tunnel.

She kicked back a buried piñon pine cone which had floated down the canyon in a long-ago flood. A flake of petrified wood which had eroded into the canyon from a stony log on top of the mesa joined the pine cone. In the dark, a broken pottery cup handle decorated with black triangles hit the pile in a shower of sand and gravel. Again and again the rat shoveled sand and debris backward

until the tunnel was totally plugged. Then she tamped the sand tight with her front paws. She was safe now -- and the snake would have to turn around in order to get back to the surface.

Feeling her way with long twitching whiskers, the kangaroo rat moved through the tunnels past the seed storage room where each night she emptied, then carefully groomed, her cheek pouches. Seeds of all kinds -- grass, dock, lupine, rabbitbrush, sagebrush and piñon pine-- nearly filled the cavity.

A cool breeze sifted into the tunnel as she approached an exit to the outside of the mound. She pattered up the passageway to the surface to poke her nose out the opening. Sniffing deeply, she looked cautiously around for predators. Golden mules-ear flowers and a desert star-lily glowed in the evening light, but nothing moved. Satisfied, she groomed the dust from her silky fur, then leaped away to find dinner, her tracks joining caterpillar, insect and mouse tracks that criss-crossed the sand like lace.

97

Ancient Artisans

Artisan = a person who makes things with artistic skill

Ancestral Puebloans made their world beautiful. They even wove beautiful patterns into the soles of their sandals where they didn't show. Children practiced crafts from the time they were toddlers. Most hunters could probably flake their own arrowheads -- they'd been practicing since they were young.

Small children sat beside adults and made baskets, pots or cloth -- awkwardly at first, but better in time. Some were more skilled at weaving or cooking, some at hunting or farming corn, beans and squash. People did what they could do best.

A cracked cooking pot could be mended with melted pine pitch then used as a storage pot. Other mending was also common (see below). Mended pottery was often placed in graves. Broken pieces (potsherds) became scoops or spoons, pot scrapers, gambling tokens, jar lids, or necklace pendants. Pieces with beautiful designs were probably saved (as they are now) to use as patterns for new pot decorations. Other pieces were ground into powder and used to make more pots.

Warp and Weft

In weaving, vertical fibers are called the "warp" and the fibers that go back and forth are called the "weft." The cliff dwellers wove juniper bark, yucca and plant stem fibers, animal wool and fur, milkweed fluff, and cotton (first cultivated by tribes in southern Arizona) on their looms.

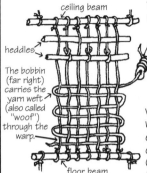

ceiling beam
heddles
The bobbin (far right) carries the yarn weft (also called "woof") through the warp.
floor beam

Fibers were dyed, using plant parts and berries for the various colors. Designs were painted on, and even ancient tie-dyed cloth has been found. Clothing was woven the size and shape needed for wearing, so that when it was taken off the loom the fibers wouldn't have to be cut.

Yucca and strips of rabbit fur were twined together then woven into highly prized warm, heavy blankets for use on cold nights.

Sandals, net baskets and belts were knotted or plaited (woven without a loom). Grass bundles were bound together with juniper fibers to make kneeling, sitting and sleeping pads.

Redrock Grocery List

corn: roasted fresh, dried or ground.
beans: eaten fresh or dried, stored.
squash: eaten fresh or sliced thin and dried.
meat (mammals and birds): eaten raw or cooked, or sliced thin and dried.
yucca (mostly *baccata* pods, petals, stems and new leaves): eaten raw, baked, boiled, ground, dried, made into juice, stored. Roots made a kind of soap.
seeds (grasses, amaranth, sagebrush, pepper grass, sunflower, etc.): roasted, ground for meal or used as seasoning, stored for later use.
wild berries and fruits: fresh or cooked, ground or chopped, dried in cakes, juiced, used for flavoring.
cactus: eaten fresh, cooked, or mashed and dried.
wild onion: fresh, cooked or dried, as seasoning.
roots: eaten fresh, cooked or sliced and dried.
nuts (piñon, acorn): eaten ripe, roasted, mashed and made into cakes, stored, as seasoning.

Whodunnit?

Interpreting the past takes good detective work. We *think* Ancestral Puebloan women made the pottery because Pueblo women do now. But maybe the men did. We only know that the potters were very skilled. In fact, the coiled cooking pots made with rough corrugations heated food better than the iron pots used by more "advanced" cultures.

We *think* men did the weaving since in villages with kivas (underground ceremonial rooms which, in modern Hopi villages, are used mostly by men) looms were built into the walls. But it's possible that women wove cloth in the ancient kivas. Or maybe women once wove cloth but it later became a task for men. It's impossible to be certain, but it's fun to search for clues.

OOPS!

A cracked pot could be mended by drilling small holes on each side of the crack, lacing the edges together with yucca twine, and, if needed, waterproofing it with pine pitch.

Housewares

"Seed jars" held small things like seeds, beads, or other small treasures. Holes for thongs allowed them to be carried or hung in a safe spot.

The stone blade of a knife was glued into a slot in the wooden handle with pine pitch.

A coiled cooking pot was built to last. Its rough surface caught and held the heat.

A cup or pitcher might have a fancy animal handle.

Cottonwood slabs made lightweight serving trays or plates.

Spirits and Gods

What do we really *know* about the spiritual life of the cliff dwellers? We're pretty sure they believed in life after death because they left pots full of food in burial pits, apparently for use by the dead in the afterworld.

Some petroglyphs and pictographs may have had religious or spiritual meanings because we know rock art has religious meaning in other cultures all around the world. Perhaps the artists were drawing their visions or dreams.

But that doesn't mean that *all* rock art is religious -- some artists may have been recording history or making maps. Or maybe a cliff-dwelling artist just had an itch to sketch!

Chapter 48. The Ancient Artisans

perhaps...

The red canyon echoes with the voices of ancient Puebloans going about their business.

An elder sits rolling stringy juniper bark along his thigh. His gnarled fingers add new lengths of bark, creating a strong, twisted cord like the one that keeps a nearby turkey from wandering. He hums as he works....

Nearby, a man unrolls a long mat made of willow sticks. Inside are warp beams, heddles, bobbins and a beater -- a portable loom ready to set up for weaving....

A potter presses a long roll of clay onto the rim of a new pot with fingers and thumb. She plans the beautiful design she will paint on it....

A teenager on the mesa above the village sits cross-legged, flaking an arrow point. He stops to scan the horizon for raiders that might try to attack the village....

Resting on a grass mat, a man sips herbal tea from a mug. Putting it aside, he scoops up pats of freshly mixed mud-and-weedstems from an old basket and carefully sets a stone in the wall he is building....

Young women chant corn songs as they grind corn with manos in stone metates. A girl crushes grass seeds with a pestle in a deep hollow worn into the ledge....

Youngsters scramble up the final ladder to the village with long-necked pots full of water and a net basket filled with spicy peppergrass and sagebrush seeds for making scented sage-cakes....

Giggling children mix colored dust with grease, and paint each other with frayed yucca-stem brushes. A baby takes its first wobbling steps. Some girls learn a ceremonial dance from a stern elderly woman....

A running child knocks the wall-builder's cup off the ledge and it shatters on the midden below. The broken handle with four black triangles lies in the dust as the child peers over the edge in dismay....

A young man drills the final hole in a long, hollow eagle leg bone, then holds the flute to his lips and blows gently. Maybe at sunrise he will play it near the pot-holes when the girl from the visiting clan comes to fill her water jar. Will she like his song? The soft, sweet notes join a bat flitting overhead in the evening dusk....

Pallid Bat

Antrozous pallidus (an-troh-ZOH-us PAL-id-us)
antro = "cave"   *zous* = "dweller"   *pallidus* = "pale"

The rimrock mesas provide lots of places for bats to live. The pallid bat, with its 15" wingspan, is one of the largest bats in the redrock country. It begins foraging at dusk and flies near the ground -- sometimes only three to six feet up -- with slow, strong wingbeats (most other bats flit around like bits of black paper in a lively breeze). Since it is one of the few bats that makes a noise that humans can hear -- a buzzy rasping sound -- you'll probably notice when a pallid bat flies by.

Unlike other bats, the bold pallid bat sometimes lands on the ground to forage. It has been known to pin a 5" scorpion to the ground with teeth and thumbs, then kill and eat it.

Day roosts are usually cracks in the rock. Night roosts are in more open areas, like cave ceilings. The pallid bat can take quite a bit of cold and heat, and has been recorded active between 0° and 25° C. (that's between 32° and 80° F.). It probably hibernates, but we don't know much about that.

SHHH !!!

Hey, look! There's a cave! Let's explore! First, peek inside. No bears, no cougars or bobcats...so it's okay to go in. Right? Wait -- look again. If you see any dark bumps hanging from the ceiling, back off.

Some bats gather, or roost, in caves. If baby bats are there, it's a *maternity* (muh-TUR-nih-tee) roost. You can endanger a bat colony by disturbing a roost. Scared bats crash around, knocking babies to the floor where they will die. (You can't save them.) If adults fly from the cave in the daylight, they'll probably be grabbed by ravens or hawks -- then their babies will starve.

You might even endanger *yourself*. How? Sometimes frightened bats pee on intruders, which is BAD news -- viruses in their urine can make you sick enough to kill you.

So don't just rush into caves. Always check for bat colonies first.

SOund NAvigation Ranging

SO-NA-R. That's where the word **sonar** comes from. "Sonar" usually refers to underwater activities but sometimes it is used to describe the method bats use to navigate in the air.

A better word is echolocation, which means finding things by hearing the echo made when sound hits an object and bounces back to you. Bats can detect something the size of a bumblebee from fifteen feet away!

A bat's clicks and squeaks are extremely noisy -- as loud (really) as a jet plane or a subway train -- but usually higher on the scale than the human ear can hear. The echoes of the loud clicks give strong, very detailed messages that the bat can interpret as shapes, sizes and distances.

Hang IN There, Baby!

A birthing mother bat hangs upright from her thumbs and her baby is born into the cup of her wings and tail. The newborn baby grabs a nipple in its mouth and hangs on like a bulldog! Wouldn't you?

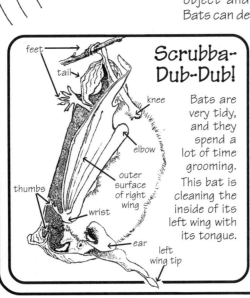

Scrubba-Dub-Dub!

feet
tail
knee
elbow
thumbs
outer surface of right wing
wrist
ear
left wing tip

Bats are very tidy, and they spend a lot of time grooming. This bat is cleaning the inside of its left wing with its tongue.

The Frightful Solifugid

Solifugid (sol-ih-FEW-jid -- also called *solpugid*) means "running from the sun." The jaws of this swift-moving, inch-long, hairy spider relative are huge, and it can give quite a nip, but it doesn't inject venom (poison). The front pair of "legs" are actually feelers called *pedipalps* (*pedi* = foot, *palp* = feeler). They help it hold prey.

Solifugids are carnivorous -- they hunt and eat whatever moves -- up to the size of baby mice and lizards. Scary, huh?

Chapter 49. The Pallid Bat

The female pallid bat, flying low above some datura flowers, detected the sphinx moth with her clicking sonar. With a quick swoop, she snagged the moth. It struggled wildly, which would have frightened off most bats -- but not the big pallid bat!

Dropping to the sand with her heavy meal, she nipped off the moth's head and snipped off the wings and let them drop. Then she chewed and swallowed the soft abdomen. As she finished, a tiny pink newborn bat that was attached to her nipple stretched its filmy wings then snuggled closer to its mother. Pallid bat babies are usually left to hang in the colony when the mothers go out to hunt, but they may be taken along for the ride.

She reached down to nose the baby, making sure it was well-attached, then with strong wingbeats she rose into the air again for more hunting. As she flew, she made clicking sounds and listened for the echoes that bounced off rocks and plants and insects. She could tell what each echo meant, and she overtook and caught several medium-sized moths, then landed to pounce on and eat a hairy solifugid scuttling across a rock.

The sonar of many bats cannot be heard, but the pallid bat had a high-pitched clicking buzz that blended in with the many night sounds of the red rock canyon. It clicked along with the chirps of the crickets, a grasshopper mouse squealing its tiny howl, the *"waa-waa-waa"* of the spadefoot toad, and the great horned owl's deep *"whooo, hu-hoo, hooo."* It buzzed along with the coughing *"arghk! arghk!"* of the gray fox and the *"wup-wup-wah-eeeer"* of the coyote as it sang to the moon.

At dawn, the pallid bat headed for her roost just below the canyon rim. Her clicks beat time with the *"tee tee tee tee tee tee"* of the white-throated swifts and the early *"kooo-ooo-ah!.... koooooo····koookooo"* of the mourning doves. Ravens greeted the day with a *"BRONK! RONK!"* Canyon wrens filled the canyon with their musical *"ti-ti-ti-tui-tui-tui-tui-tooh."*

And far away, so distant that perhaps it wasn't even there, came a soft sound -- almost like a flute -- from the ancient cliff dwellings of the side canyon.....

♪♪♫♩♩♪♪♪♪♪♩♪♩♪♪♪♪,♪♪♩♪♪♪

In the redrock canyon country, life goes on.

The End

Stop the Invasion!

Most people who love animals don't want to see them destroyed. But what if the animals they love are demolishing or crowding out native wildlife or habitats? Here are some solutions:

*There are hormone inoculation (in-ock-yew-LAY-shun -- injection) programs to prevent feral (FAIR-ull --once domesticated but now living wild) animals from producing young. This doesn't harm the animals, they just don't have offspring, and when they die naturally the problem ends with them.

*The government has a program to help people adopt wild horses and burros which over-graze range and badly affect native wildlife and habitat.

*There are programs to pull up and get rid of weed plants that are crowding out native plants.

*Many other things can be done to help, too, and volunteers are often needed. Call your local agencies and ask what you can do to help. They're in the phone book.

Canyon Aliens (to name a few...)

Cheatgrass...cattle...tamarisk...brook trout...puncture-vine...starling...bull thistle...shiner...tumbleweed...Russian-olive...clover...horse...Scotch thistle...sheep...yellow starthistle...English sparrow...purple loosestrife...burro...Bermudagrass...silverleaf nightshade...chukar...quackgrass...brown trout...bindweed...rainbow trout...leafy spurge...chub...perennial sorghum...sculpin...perennial pepperweed...pothole midge...Canada thistle...four kinds of knapweed...goat...Johnsongrass...foxtail...and many more aliens threaten our wildlife and their habitats. And speaking of things that threaten our wildlife and habitats --- you *could* add humans to the list........

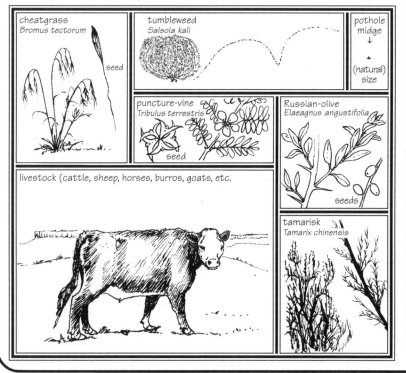

cheatgrass
Bromus tectorum
seed

tumbleweed
Salsola kali

pothole midge
↓
•
(natural) size

puncture-vine
Tribulus terrestris
seed

Russian-olive
Elaeagnus angustifolia
seeds

livestock (cattle, sheep, horses, burros, goats, etc.

tamarisk
Tamarix chinensis

Aliens Are USING *YOU*!

How much of a problem are aliens? Watch for them when you hike where horses, burros or llamas have used the trail. What you'll see is what they eat -- and poop along the trail -- **cheatgrass, clover, various grasses, alfalfa.** All aliens.

Look out over grassy hillsides in early summer. Is the hillside covered with short blond grass? It's probably cheat-grass. Check out streambanks. Are they lined with trees that look like short, feathery, messy willows? In spring do they have beautiful pink flower masses? That's **tamarisk.** Or maybe you see a silvery-green willowy tree with yellowish olive-shaped fruits. Another alien -- this one is called **Russian-olive**, although it isn't a *real* olive. It crowds out natives, too. For others, see the list.

Native plants and animals aren't frail and helpless. They are perfectly adapted to live in their environment. But they may not have the particular "skills" needed to combat an invader. They may grow too slowly, mature later, or maybe their roots can't compete with an invader's larger, stronger roots.

With wildlife, perhaps their food gets eaten by hungry invaders. Perhaps caution that helps them avoid danger also keeps them from competing.

Some native plants and animals can adapt to intruders through changes in their habits or through genetic changes. Others can't.

So. What do you do when you go for a walk or hike and return with seeds stuck in your socks? You pick them off and toss them. Right? WAIT!

Here's how YOU can slow the alien invasion. Next time, pick the seeds off but put them in a trash can, or in your campfire if you're camping -- or even in your pocket until you have a good place to get rid of them without helping them spread. That way you won't be "used" by the aliens to find a new home!

Chapter 50. The "Aliens"

There are **aliens** living in the canyon country -- "moved-in-ers" that didn't evolve there. They are animals and plants that have been brought in purposely by people, were carried in on car tires, arrived in livestock feed or droppings, or came in other ways.

Most people don't have a clue that anything is wrong. The aliens look right at home -- happy and healthy. Unless you knew what it was like before they came, you might think they'd been there forever.

Take cheatgrass, for example. Cheatgrass is an *annual* grass, meaning it grows, makes seeds, and dies by midsummer. Next spring, the seeds sprout and it starts again. Cheatgrass came from Europe and is now found all over the United States. The seeds stick in your socks if you walk through it. On the open range it takes over, pushing out native *perennials* (pur-EN-ee-ulz -- plants that stay green from year to year) and spreading its pretty golden blanket over the landscape. What's wrong with that? The cheatgrass is dry and worthless as food by the end of summer instead of fresh and green like the native grasses that were crowded out. So the native animals go hungry -- "cheated" out of their winter food.

The cheatgrass came in animal feed -- hay and straw and grain -- for the last 150 years. It has been spread far and wide in livestock droppings. Every seed that gets dropped in a cowpie (that's another name for cattle scat) gets off to a great start with a big plop of fertilizer. After that, they spread themselves. Even now cheatgrass and other crop seeds get spread to new areas in feed and droppings of cows, sheep, goats, horses, burros, llamas and wildlife.

Horses and burros are alien *animals*. Burros in the canyon country are *feral* -- wild offspring of animals that were once domesticated. The burros eat food needed by wildlife such as deer, bighorn sheep, and even ground squirrels and kangaroo rats. People like burros and don't want to see them removed from the range, but burros don't really belong there and they don't get along with the wildlife. Burros like to wade in and muddy up waterholes but bighorn sheep won't come to a waterhole if burros are around, so they are driven away by burro populations. Since bighorns are having trouble surviving anyway, this puts their lives in danger.

Cattle like to hang around in streambeds. They trample them so badly that all the plants die. Without the shade from vegetation, water evaporates from the hot soil. Many streams dry up and the streambanks erode and cut deeply into the ground. It may take years for a stream to recover after cattle have damaged it. That makes wildlife survival tough.

Sheep and goats eat all parts of a plant, including the roots and fresh buds on trees and shrubs. A landscape grazed by sheep and goats may be eaten down to bare earth, leaving little or nothing for wildlife.

Some aliens are escapees. Burros and horses escaped from prospectors. Fishermen lose or dump alien fish and crayfish used as bait (plus their diseases and parasites) into streams from their bait buckets. Alien birds like starlings take over nest sites.

Sometimes people introduce plants or animals on purpose. The government has introduced some really awful aliens into the environment -- with good intentions, of course. They thought the tamarisk tree would help keep river and stream banks from washing away. It did, but it also has crowded out many native plants necessary to the survival of wildlife -- and it makes an impassable tangle along most western streams, particularly in the desert. It's still spreading out of control. Government agencies like the U.S. Forest Service and the Bureau of Land Management are learning that they need to test things before introducing them into new environments, but mistakes are still being made. A lot of tax dollars are spent correcting these errors.

"Alien invasions" can happen anywhere. Dogs and cats running free chase and kill a lot of wildlife -- even in our suburban yards. Landscape plants like pampas grass and bamboo take over acres of wildlife habitat when they or their seeds escape into some wild areas.

People can help by making sure they don't let new plants or animals escape into wild habitats. Unwanted pets should never be "released" to fend for themselves -- feral cats dumped beside roads around the country kill *gazillions* of wild birds and native wildlife every year just to survive. Get the picture?

Don't despair -- just be aware!

Hiking and Camping

Canyon Campsites
If you camp in a canyon, don't sleep in the sandy bottom even if it's dry. Flash floods can happen day or night. Pick a spot well up the side of the canyon above debris from previous floods.

Look for jumbled heaps of twigs, branches and juniper bark, sand banks that have been sliced away by water so that you can see a cross-section (a cutbank), and clumps of weeds and juniper bark caught in branches. Search well -- they could be 15' up! **Put your tent or sleeping bag above this line.** If you do hear a rumble, day or night, quickly move high above the flood line.

Mini-Dracula
Ticks hang around on wildlife and plants. They grab you as you pass by, dig in, suck and swell up with your blood. You may not even feel it!

hungry ticks

all natural size

full tick

Ticks spread disease, so after hiking, check your whole body for ticks. Remove them by pulling gently -- be sure to get the head, too -- then apply antiseptic.

Grazing On The Goodies
There are several reasons why you shouldn't pick flowers or eat (graze) wild food, like berries or cactus fruits, in the canyon country, even if they are pretty or edible (not poisonous). Here are some reasons:

1. Wildlife may be depending on those berries or fruits for survival -- you can always make it back to camp or to a grocery store for **your** food. They can't.

2. The plant's flowers or fruits are there for making seeds. If you pick them, their seeds will not grow into new plants or make food for wildlife. The plants won't be there to protect the soil against erosion. And that plant might be on the endangered list -- you can't tell just by looking.

3. You may be allergic to flowers and fruits that aren't harmful to animals or other people. Don't take a chance.

4. It is against the law to pick flowers or fruits in most national parks, monuments, or other protected areas.

5. YOU wouldn't like it if people had picked all the flowers before YOU got there!

My Dog is Perfect
Maybe at home it is. But just imagine how the wildlife you read about in this book must feel when your **genuinely nice dog** comes trotting up the trail. Dogs are chasers and hunters. They will joyfully bark at, chase, catch and eat just about ANY animal they find. And that's not fair. Please leave your dog at home when you visit wild places. If you can't leave it home, be sure to keep it on a leash, clean up its poop, and <u>don't let it bark</u>!

I WANT That!
If you see interesting things when you're in the canyon country, you may want to collect them and take them home with you.

Don't do it. Most of those things are protected by law. If you are caught with them you may get fined Big Time (this happens frequently, by the way). Unless you have a special permit, it's against the law:

*to carry away artifacts like arrowheads or pottery pieces
*to remove fossils from most places
*to have bird feathers in your possession
*to pick or disturb an endangered plant
*to write or make marks (*graffiti*) on rock faces

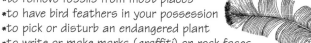

In national parks and monuments it's even against the rules to take home a pretty rock. "If everyone took one there wouldn't be any left," they tell us. We'd rather not hear it, but it's probably true.

If you like to collect things, collect **pictures** with a camera. You can make a great photo collection to show all your friends, and pictures take up less room than a collection. There are other interesting things you can do, too -- see <u>Things To Do,</u> on pages 106 and 107.

Besides, did you ever notice? Souvenirs in the box under your bed never again seem quite as terrific as they did when you first discovered them in their natural surroundings.

Going Hiking
You're ready to go! The sun is warm, nice breeze, lots of neat rocks to climb and, yeah! you're ready to go. Wait -- are you REALLY ready? If you want to have a great hike, don't race off without a few important things. A small backpack or fanny pack may carry what you need. Here's a checklist:

full water bottle -- *if you take only ONE thing, take this*
sunscreen -- put some on *before* you leave, then take it along
sun glasses -- UV in desert sunlight *can harm your eyes*
energy bar -- granola or chocolate
lunch -- if you'll be gone long. Don't take stuff that will spoil if it gets hot. Oranges stay cool and fresh and they're juicy. Remember to bring the peels back with you.
a whistle -- to call for help if you break your leg or get lost
light windbreaker or rain jacket (the kind you can scrunch up into a little ball and stick in your pocket) In winter, carry a foil emergency blanket. Weather can change **suddenly.**
bug repellent -- mosquitoes and no-see-ums can eat you alive
hiking boots -- sandals or smooth soles aren't a good idea
bandaids or moleskin -- in case you start to get a blister
hat with a brim -- to shade your eyes and keep your brain from getting scrambled like fried eggs in the sun
map and compass -- if you're going to go very far
tissue -- in a plastic bag (*see next page for good advice*)

If you are interested and don't mind the extra weight:
binoculars, camera and extra film -- protect film from heat
ID (identification) guides -- birds, geology, flowers, insects, reptiles and amphibians, mammals, etc.
a little notebook and pen/pencil -- for writing stuff down

Being Snake Savvy

You probably won't ever see a rattler. Western rattlesnakes are timid, and try to hide from danger. So you need to avoid where they are hiding, and not surprise them. If you follow these simple rules, you should be safe.

Snakes hide in cool places, beneath rocks or in rodent burrows when it is hot, and seek warm places at night or when it is cool. They may sun themselves on rocks early in the morning in summer or during the day on chilly spring or autumn days. They like to lie on warm sand after dark.

1. Wear shoes or boots, not sandals. Most snake bites occur below the knee.

2. Don't reach into dark places without first looking carefully. Fingers and arms make good targets.

3. Don't climb anywhere you can't see to check for snakes first. They may not coil or rattle before striking.

4. Look carefully before stepping across a rock or log if there is room for a snake to hide on the far side.

5. If hiking on a warm night use a flashlight and wear boots. Try to finish hikes before dark.

6. If you meet a snake, hold perfectly still until it loses interest and moves away. If you must move, do it very slowly. Make a wide detour around more distant snakes.

7. If sleeping outdoors, zip your tent shut. Snakes like warm places and may try to snuggle up to you.

8. If you are bitten, don't panic and run. This makes your blood pump faster, circulating the poison more quickly. Tie a string or scarf around the arm or leg (or whatever) between the bite and the heart -- just tight enough to indent the skin and block the poison without cutting off the blood supply.

9. If you are alone, walk slowly to a place where you can get help and be taken to a hospital. If someone is with you, they should bring help to carry you out if necessary. If you can, apply ice to the bite until you arrive at the hospital.

Snakebites may not be fatal. Small children and frail or elderly adults may be at risk, but snakes often don't inject much, if any, poison when they bite and victims almost always survive. Many doctors feel snakebite kits cause more damage than snake bites, so use a kit at your own risk.

OH, GROSS! Have you ever found a place where somebody went to the toilet outdoors? ICK! But what if you *have* to "go"? Here are some tips to help you Leave No Trace:

When hiking, *always* carry a "potty kit" in your pocket. In a sealable plastic bag, put about six feet of toilet tissue folded up small. Also enclose another small plastic bag into which you can put used tissues. Gotta go? Find a spot at least 200' from any water, where no one is likely to walk and where the next heavy rain or flashflood won't wash it out. Check for scorpions, centipedes and spiders. With a trowel or a stick, dig a "cathole" about six inches deep and six inches wide. Use it. When finished, push the dirt back into the hole and hide the spot with leaves or natural debris (remember, Leave No Trace). Don't drop the used tissue into the hole -- tuck it into the second plastic bag and put it back into your potty kit. If you leave the tissue in the hole it might be dug up by animals, and this would *definitely* look bad. If you only need to pee, you don't need to dig a hole. Dispose of your used tissues back at camp or the car.

Leave No Trace

People who really care about the wild country practice "Leave No Trace" camping and hiking skills and ethics. Leaving No Trace means acting in ways and doing things so that you don't leave behind any clues that you were there. In a way, it's a terrific hide-and-seek game. It's fun to pretend that someone is trying to find you, and that you aren't leaving any signs behind for them to discover. But it's really more than a game. Since so many people visit wild places, if they DON'T make an effort to clean up after themselves (or not make messes in the first place), hikes in wild places will be just like walking in a big campground through other people's' messy campsites and past the smelly toilets. Yuk!

Here are some Leave No Trace tactics.

When hiking on trails: walk single file so you don't widen or break down the trail. Don't make extra trails off to the side.

When hiking off trails: walk lightly, on rocks or sand if you can, and especially not on vegetation. If the ground is covered with cryptobiotic soil (see page 4) walk somewhere else, or don't even go there. Never walk in a permanent stream -- you will destroy the aquatic ecosystem and habitat of thousands of tiny but important plants and animals.

Camping: pick a camping spot at least 200' away from water (that's 70 - 80 footsteps) on a sandy spot without vegetation if possible. If you camp too close to water, wildlife may be afraid to come drink. Don't dig or build stone firepits and don't turn rocks over. Leave your campsite as you found it (or cleaner if someone else trashed it before you).

Campfires: It's best to use a camp stove. In some places, campfires are against the law. If you need a campfire, use only dead, fallen wood no bigger than your wrist. Don't take wood, even dead wood, from living trees. Break it, don't cut it, and don't use all the wood around your campsite. Burn wood all the way to ashes, then scatter them over a wide area away from camp. Remember, Leave No Trace!

Using water: Remember, water is precious in the desert and canyon country. Dip only clean containers into streams or pools (don't take more than you really need -- this is the wildlife's drinking water), and wash dishes or discard used water at least 200' from the water. Don't pollute it with soap, toothpaste, skin lotions, salt from sweat, food particles from dirty dishes, poop or pee, or anything else. Such pollution could make the water undrinkable, and it might kill the small organisms that live there (see page 70).

When you gotta "go": (see below)

folded tissue

second bag

sealable bag

To learn more about Leave No Trace outdoor skills and ethics look for pamphlets at Park Information Centers, go to www.lnt.org on the web, or call 1-800-332-4100.

Things To Do

Ancient Puebloan things

*Cliff Dwelling Make a model of a cliff dwelling using mud, sticks and stones. See pages 53, 55, 59 and 99.

*Face Painting Collect colored sand from places you travel. Grind it to powder between two rocks like the Indians did. Mix with sunscreen to make face paints with the different colors (it washes right off). What else can you do with different sand colors? How about a "sand painting" with colored sand? Maybe you could paint designs on cloth?

*Juniper Beads Look underneath juniper trees (see page 38) for juniper seeds with one end nipped off by squirrels. The cliff dwellers made necklaces with them (and Navajos still do). How do you suppose they made the second hole? What do you think they used for string?

Animal things

*Making Tracks Make plaster casts of animal tracks. See **Making Tracks** on page 107.

*Eye Spy After dark sit very quietly for awhile, then turn on your flashlight and look quickly around for eyeshine from ringtails, mice and woodrats, kangaroo rats, raccoons, foxes and who KNOWS what else! See page 74.

*Birdwatching Go for a walk with a bird guide book and binoculars, and watch for birds. This is a hobby you can practice almost anywhere. See many pages in this book.

*Mound Thumping Find a mound with several exit holes. Thump on it lightly with two fingers to see if there is a kangaroo rat inside who will thump back. See page 96-97.

*Woodrat Nest Explore a woodrat nest. Watch out for cactus spines! What did the rats use for building materials (see page 24)? Look for skulls and bones. Record your finds.

*Circle Survey With a stick, lightly draw a 50' circle around a juniper tree or other main attraction like a pothole. Spend one hour exploring EVERYTHING inside the circle. Record everything in your journal and try to identify plants, animals, burrows, scat, trails, insects. Draw pictures to help you remember later. Write good descriptions. Don't step on clues! See page 90 for hole ID.

Critter Squeaker

Make a grass blade "squeaker," sit quietly and blow on it at dusk, dawn, midday and after dark to see what comes to investigate.

<u>You will need:</u>   *a wide blade of grass 3-4" long

                   *two thumbs (your own, of course)

1. Place the grass blade between the edges of your thumbs and press tightly together. Keep your thumbnails facing you.
2. Blow hard into the space between your thumbs, straight in past the grass blade. The resulting sound whould be a sort of raspy squeal.

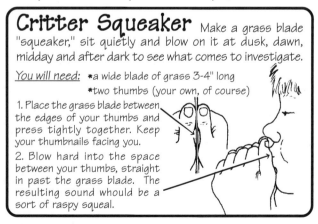

Insect things

*Owl Pellets Soak an owl pellet in warm water. See how many kinds of bones you can find. Don't worry -- it's totally sanitary, cleaned by digestive acids. A pellet may contain several different critters. See **A Bit About Bones** page 107.

*Shed Skins Hunt for a "shed" snake or lizard skin. It will be almost transparent, and probably caught in a shrub or between rocks. Can you tell what kind of reptile was once inside? See pages 66 and 82.

*Night Visitors Smooth the sand in an area where you have found tracks. Check it the next morning for fresh animal tracks. Explore sand dunes for interesting track stories. Can you figure out who did what? See page 84.

*Dove Coos Learn how to coo like a dove on page 92.

Insect things

*Grilled Bugs Check your vehicle grill for insects. Record what you find. Try to identify unsquished insects. Film containers make good storage bottles. Poke little holes in the lids to prevent mold and to let specimens dry out.

*Doodlebug Pit Scoop up a doodlebug (ant lion larva) in a cup, making sure to scoop down at least an inch below the bottom of the sand funnel. If you hold still, the doodlebug will begin to circle and make its pit. If you feel brave, put the doodlebug and some sand into your cupped hand. It will try to make its pit right in your hand (after it burrows down a bit, you'll feel it circling on your palm. It won't bite unless you hurt it). Be sure to release it where you got it, or in a similar sandy, shady place. See page 50.

*Insect Thermometer If you have a watch, you can use cricket chirps to learn the temperature. Learn how to do it on page 58.

Plant things

*Leaf Rubbings Place a leaf on a flat, hard surface. Cover it with a sheet of thin paper or a page in your journal. With a pencil or crayon, scribble back and forth over the place where the leaf is. The shape of the leaf will appear on the paper. Identify it from a plant ID (identification) book or ask someone who knows plants.

oak leaf

*Plantwatching Take a flower or tree guide on a hike and do some plantwatching. Wildflower checklists are available in some park and monument visitor centers.

Earth and Other things

*Layer Cake Study rock layers and colors as you travel. There are geology books available for many areas (see References for the Curious, page 109) and if you can identify even ONE layer, you can often figure out what many of the others are. Decide whether, or what kind of, fossils might be found in each layer. Also see pages 4-6 and 112.

*Contour Maps Study and learn how to read contour or topographic maps, available at hiking stores and park visitor centers. The map legend gives you mileages, measurements, and the elevation, in feet, between the lines on a contour map. Just for fun, take a walk and make your own contour map using five or ten foot elevations. Learn more about contour or "topo" maps inside the front cover.

*Hike-ometer Use a dollar bill (it's almost exactly six inches long) to mark off a measuring stick. Use the stick to measure how many steps you take in a hundred feet. Count your steps on a hike to know how far you went.

For example: if you hike 8,575 steps and take about 50 steps per 100 feet

Divide the number of steps you hike by how many steps you take in 100 feet. Multiply by 100 = how many feet you hike Divide by 5,280 = how many miles you hike

$8575 \div 50 = 171.5 \times 100 = 17150$
$17150 \div 5280 = 3.24$ or $3\frac{1}{4}$ miles

*BOOM! Tell people how far away lighting strikes are. Impress them with your great skill. See page 84.

*Nature Lookabout How many plant things can you <u>see</u>, <u>smell</u>, <u>hear</u> and <u>feel</u>? How many *animal* things? How long a list can you make?

Save It Forever

*Keep a Journal To save your memories forever, keep a journal -- just for yourself or to share with others. An ordinary spiral notebook works great. Write and draw pictures of interesting things you see or things you imagine. Include photos if you want. Write a poem. Paste in leaves, flowers and picture postcards. Later, every time you read your journal, you can live your redrock canyon adventure all over again!

*Photography An inexpensive recyclable camera is excellent for beginners, because you don't have to worry about losing or bashing it -- the entire camera is returned for processing. Take a camera/roll of unimportant pictures and get them developed BEFORE you're ready to take more important ones (like, on your vacation where you can't return for another shot if the first one is no good). Look at your results. If some of them aren't so great, try to figure out what happened so you won't have the same problem again. Ask the person at the camera counter (or at a camera store) if you don't understand why a photo didn't turn out well. Become your family photographer.

*Record a Hike Go hiking. Take a photo of the scene ahead every 100 steps (plus other interesting things you see). Put the photos in the correct order in a scrapbook, with descriptions and captions.

*Photo Log Make a trip log, taking snapshots of places you stay overnight. Take photos of things that interest you. Jot down dates and locations in your log and leave empty places for the photos. If you have a chance, take your film to a 1-hour processor while still on your trip and get it developed. Paste the photos in. Be sure to label them. Get your family into the pictures, too.

Making Tracks

You will need:
* fresh animal tracks
* plaster of Paris
* clean stirring stick
* water in container with lid
* empty milk carton (mold)
* an old toothbrush
* paper cup or small yogurt container

1. Cut the top and bottom off a milk carton, flatten it, and cut it as shown in the picture. Half gallon cartons make big molds, quart or pint cartons make small molds. (Practice steps 2 - 6 on a so-so track before you try to save your first really ***good*** track.)

2. Remove twigs or trash from the track and press the mold about ¼ - ½" into the ground around the track.

3. Fill the paper cup ⅞ full of dry plaster of Paris, then add about ⅓ cup water. Quickly stir until it is about as thick as pancake batter (with no lumps!). Add more water or plaster of Paris if you need to, but hurry -- it hardens fast!

4. Gently pour plaster into the mold about ¾ inch thick. Note the time. As it sets, it will heat up. But after 20 minutes it will cool and be nearly hard. Leave it as long as you can -- an hour is best if you have time to wait.

5. Lift it up, slide off the mold, and wash off the dirt. Brush clean with a toothbrush, but don't scratch it. Ink the track with a felt-tip pen to make it show up better.

6. Identify the track using an animal-track field guide. Write identification, date, and location on it.

A Bit About Bones

In dry habitats, bones last a long time. You may find bones around woodrat nests, in owl pellets (see page 52), or just lying on the ground. Most animals have similarly shaped bones for similar purposes so, except for size, a bobcat leg bone looks much like a mouse's, a deer rib looks much like a coyote's, and so on. Here are some of the most common shapes. Not all the bones shown below are natural size.

<u>**rib:**</u> long, curved, flat or cylindrical, with a knob on one end to connect to the vertebra

<u>**vertebra:**</u> chunky, with a hole through the center and sharp "fins." A tail vertebra has no hole -- it looks like a little drum. So does a fish vertebra. Fish bones are semi-transparent.

<u>**leg:**</u> long, cylindrical with a knob on each end, sometimes with a skinny sidebone.

<u>**toe:**</u> short and straight sometimes with a slight knob on each end.

<u>**pelvis:**</u> has a large hole, plus a socket for the leg to fit in.

<u>**scapula (shoulder blade):**</u> looks like a fan with a ridge down the back.

<u>**skull:**</u> *herbivore* teeth are snippers and grinders, while *carnivore* teeth are snappers and rippers. (That must mean carnivorous grasshopper mice snap and rip with their snippers and grinders...?)

woodrat skull   bobcat skull

References for the Curious

Note: Most or all of these books are still in print. If not, maybe a bookstore can locate a copy for you.
Check web booksites like www.amazon.com.

Mammals

Field Guide to Animal Tracks, A. Murie, O., Boston: Houghton Mifflin Co., 1954

Field Guide to the Mammals, A. Burt, W. and Grossenheider, R., Boston: Houghton Mifflin Co., 1976

Mammals of the Canyon Country. Armstrong, D., Moab, UT: Canyonlands Natural History Assn., 1982

Mammals of the Intermountain West. Zeveloff, S., Salt Lake City: University of Utah Press, 1988

Mammals of the Southwest Deserts. Olin, G., Tucson, AZ: Southwest Parks & Monuments Assn., 1982

Sleek & Savage, North America's Weasel Family. Haley, D., Seattle: Pacific Search Books, 1975

Birds

Audubon Society Encyclopedia of North American Birds, The. Terres, J., New York: A. A. Knopf, 1980

Audubon Society Field Guide to North American Birds, The; Western Region. Udvardy, M., New York: A. A. Knopf, 1977

Field Guide to Western Birds, A. Peterson, R. T., Boston: Houghton Mifflin Co., 1961

Guide to Bird Behavior, A, Vol. I. Stokes, D., Boston: Little, Brown & Co., 1979

Guide to Bird Behavior, A, Vol. II. Stokes, D. and L., Boston: Little, Brown & Co., 1983

Guide to Field Identification -- Birds of North America, A. Robbins, Bruun, Zim & Singer, New York: Golden Press, 1983

Reptiles, Amphibians & Fishes

Field Guide to Freshwater Fishes, A. Page, L., and Brooks, B., Boston: Houghton Mifflin Co., 1991

Field Guide to Western Reptiles and Amphibians. Stebbins, R. A., Boston: Houghton Mifflin Co., 1966

Guide to Field Identification -- Amphibians of North America, A. Smith, H., New York: Golden Press, 1978

Guide to Field Identification -- Reptiles of North America, A. Smith, H. and Brodie, Jr., E., New York: Golden Press, 1982

Reptiles, The. Carr, A., New York: Time-Life Books, 1971

Insects, Spiders & Scorpions

Audubon Society Field Guide to North American Butterflies, The. Pyle, R., New York: A. A. Knopf, 1981

Black Widow, The. Cornett, J., Palm Springs, CA: Palm Springs Desert Museum, 1994

Field Guide to the Beetles of North America, A. White, R., Boston: Houghton Mifflin Co., 1983

Field Guide to the Insects of America North of Mexico, A. Borror, D. and White, R., Boston: Houghton Mifflin Co., 1970

Peterson First Guide to Caterpillars of North America. Wright, A., Boston: Houghton Mifflin Co., 1993

Scorpions. Billings, C., New York: Dodd, Mead & Company, 1983

Simon & Schuster's Guide to Insects. Arnett, Jr., R. and Jacques, Jr., R., New York: Simon & Schuster, 1981

Plants

Field Guide to Southwestern and Texas Wildflowers, A. Niehaus, T., Ripper, C., Savage, V., Boston, Houghton Mifflin Co., 1984

Flowers of the Canyon Country. Welsh, S. and Ratcliffe, B., Moab, UT: Canyonlands Natural History Assn., 1971

Flowers of the Southwest Mesas. Patraw, P., Globe, AZ: Southwestern Monuments Assn., 1953

North American Trees. Preston, R., Ames, IA: The Iowa State University Press, 1961

Sagebrush Country. Taylor, R., Missoula, MT: Mountain Press Publishing Co., 1992

Shrubs and Trees of the Southwest Deserts. Bowers, J. E., Tucson, AZ: S.W. Parks and Monuments Assn., 1993

Shrubs and Trees of the Southwest Uplands. Elmore, F., Tucson, AZ: Southwest Parks and Monuments Assn., 1976

Trees of North America. Brockman, F., Zim, H., and Merrilees, R., New York: Golden Press, 1968

Wildflowers of Zion National Park. Welsh, S., Springdale, UT: Zion Natural History Assn., 1990

Geology

Canyon Country Geology for the Layman and Rockhound. Barnes, F., Salt Lake City: Wasatch Publishers Inc., 1978
Field Guide to Geology, The. Lambert, D. and the Diagram Group, New York: Facts on File, 1988
Landforms -- Heart of the Colorado Plateau. Ladd, G., Las Vegas: KC Publications, 1995
Roadside Geology of Utah. Chronic, H., Missoula, MT: Mountain Press Publishing Company., 1990
    (also see **Roadside Geology** guides for other states)
Scenes of the Plateau Lands. Stokes, W., Salt Lake City: Publishers Press, 1969
Sculpturing of Zion, The. Hamilton, W., Zion National Park, UT: Zion Natural History Assn., 1984

Native Americans

American Indian Food and Lore, 150 Authentic Recipes. Niethammer, C., New York: Collier Publications, 1974
Earth, Water and Fire, The Prehistoric Pottery of Mesa Verde. Oppelt, N., Boulder, CO: Johnson Publishing Co., 1991
In Search of the Old Ones, Exploring the Anasazi World of the SW. Roberts, D., New York: Simon & Schuster, 1996
Indians of the Four Corners. Marriott, A., Santa Fe: Ancient City Press, 1996
Legacy on Stone. Cole, S., Boulder, CO: Johnson Publishing, 1990
North American Indian Art. Furst, P. & J., New York: Rizzoli International Publications, Inc., 1982
Old Ones, The, A Children's Book About the Anasazi Indians. Freeman, B. & J., Albuquerque: The Think Shop, Inc., 1986
Zuni Indians and Their Uses of Plants, The. Stevenson, M.C., New York: Dover Publications, 1993 (orig. 1915)

Miscellaneous Books

American Wildlife & Plants -- A Guide to Wildlife Food Habits. Martin, A., Zim, H., Nelson, A., New York: Dover, 1951
Arches, The Story Behind the Scenery. Johnson, D., Las Vegas: KC Publications, 1985
Beaver Year. Brady, I., Talent, OR: Nature Works, 1997 **(www.natureworksbooks.com)**
Desert Animals. Tate, R., New York: Harper & Row, 1971
Desert, The. Leopold, A.S., New York: Time-Life Books, 1976
Deserts, The Audubon Society Nature Guide. MacMahon, J., New York: Chanticleer Press, Inc., 1992
Desert Wildlife. Jaeger, E., Stanford, CA: Stanford University Press, 1961
Eyewitness: Skeleton. Parker, S., New York: A. A. Knopf, 1988
Field Guide to Wildlife Habitats of the Western U.S., The. Benyus, J.M., New York: Simon & Schuster, 1989
Four Corners. Brown, K., New York: HarperCollins, 1995
Guide to Capitol Reef Rocklife, A. Capitol Reef Natural History Assn., Salt Lake City: Paragon Press, 1982
House in the Sun. Olin, G., Phoenix, AZ: Southwest Parks & Monuments Assn., 1977
International Wildlife Encyclopedia, The. Burton, M. & R., New York: Marshall Cavendish Corp., 1969
Journals of Lewis & Clark, The, 2 Vol. Ed. by Biddle, N., New York: The Heritage Press, 1962
Leave No Trace. Developed and published by Outdoor Skills & Ethics, Lander, WY: 1994
National Audubon Society Field Guide to North American Weather. Ludlum, D., New York: A. A. Knopf, 1991
Nevada's Red Rock Canyon. Cinkoske, C., Las Vegas: KC Publications, 1988
Nevada's Valley of Fire. Fiero, G., Las Vegas: KC Publications, 1985
Poisonous Dwellers of the Desert. Dodge, N., Globe, AZ: Southwestern Monuments Assn., 1966
Pond Life - A Golden Guide. Reid, G., New York: Golden Press, 1967
Sierra Club Guide to the National Parks. Beasley, Jr., C. et al, New York: Steward Tabori & Chang, Inc. 1984
Sierra Club Naturalist's Guide to Deserts of the Southwest, The. Larson, P., San Francisco: Sierra Club Books, 1977
Wild Babies, A Canyon Sketchbook. Brady, I., Talent, OR: Nature Works, 1994 **(www.natureworksbooks.com)**
Zion, The Story Behind the Scenery. Eardley, A. & Schaack J., Las Vegas: KC Publications, 1989

Miscellaneous Magazines and Pamphlets

Animal and plant checklists available at park and monument visitor centers
National Geographic, Arizona Highways, Audubon, National Wildlife, Natural History, The Nature Conservancy, Defenders of Wildlife, Ranger Rick Nature Magazine, Smithsonian, Discover, Earth, ZooNooz and other magazine articles and photos.

Changing the Scenery

The **wind** is stripping away sand and soil bit by bit, removing it from where it has been for millions of years and carrying it into valleys, lakes, ponds, marshes and other protected spots where it settles in layers.

Water evaporates, depositing layers of minerals like salt and alkali.

Eons of **raindrops** wear away rocks and soil.

Flooding **rivers** carry boulders, silt and debris far beyond their banks.

Rain and **ice** loosen soil and rock, and they're carried to lower levels by **landslides.**

Volcanoes spew lava from deep inside the planet, covering older layers of earth.

Glaciers grind down mountains and valleys, leaving piles of gravel, sand and soil where they melt.

Ocean tides bring sand to the beach then remove it with every tide.

And don't forget **earthquakes, tsunamis, asteroids and humans!**

Whew! It's amazing the geological record isn't *TOTALLY* scrambled!

Anyway, now you know why some layers are missing in parts of the redrock country, and also why a certain layer may be found only in one small area.

Wind, rain, ocean tides, volcanoes, floods, freezing temperatures, glaciers, and many other forces have been at work since the beginning, rearranging the amazing world we live in.

The Geological Layer Cake

The diagram below shows the major rock layers found in the canyon country. The layers are generally in this order (you won't find the Moenkopi layer above the Entrada layer, for instance, because Moenkopi shale was laid down before Entrada sandstone).

Layers may be inches or feet thick, and in places they end, blend, or interweave with other layers, so all layers are not found in all areas. Why? Well, think about what's happening all over the earth right now (see Changing the Scenery, this page).

Natural Bridges National Monument - UT
Grand Canyon National Park - AZ
Monument Valley Navajo Tribal Park - UT & AZ
Canyon De Chelly National Monument - AZ
Valley of Fire State Park - NV
Zion National Park - UT
Navajo National Monument - AZ
Red Rock Canyon Recreation Area - NV
Rainbow Bridge National Monument - UT
Arches National Park - UT
Canyonlands National Park - UT
Hovenweep National Monument - UT & CO
El Morro National Monument - NM
Colorado National Monument - CO
Capitol Reef National Park - UT
Mesa Verde National Park - CO
Glen Canyon National Recreation Area - UT & AZ
Grand Staircase-Escalante Nat. Mon. - UT
Chaco Culture National Historical Park - NM
Bryce Canyon National Park - UT
Cedar Breaks National Monument - UT
Petrified Forest National Park - AZ

A dotted line means these layers are missing at a particular site.

The cliff model below shows the layers in correct order and where to see them

Era or Age	Period and Epoch	Formation or Layer Name
CENOZOIC ERA 0 - 65 MYA	**Tertiary** — includes Eocene, Miocene, Pliocene, Pleistocene, etc.	Brian Head (lava)
		Wasatch/Claron (limestone)
"MYA" means Million Years Ago	**Cretaceous** 65 MYA — first flowering plants appear, dinosaurs become extinct	Mesa Verde (sandstone)
		Mancos (shale)
		Dakota (sandstone)
MESOZOIC ERA 65 - 225 MYA	**Jurassic** 136 MYA — first birds appear	Morrison (mixed rock)
		Entrada (sandstone)
		Carmel (mixed rock)
		Navajo (sandstone)
		Kayenta (mixed rock)
		Wingate/Aztec (sandstone)
	Triassic 190 MYA — first dinosaurs appear, first primitive mammals appear	Chinle (mostly shale)
		Shinarump (conglomerate)
		Moenkopi (shale)
	Permian 225 MYA — mammal-like reptiles appear	White Rim (sandstone)
		Organ Rock (shale)
		Cedar Mesa (sandstone)
		Halgaito (shale)
PALEOZOIC ERA 225-570 MYA	**Pennsylvanian** 280 MYA — first reptiles appear	Honaker Trail (sandstone/limestone)
		Paradox Evaporites (salt)
	Mississippian 325 MYA	Molas (conglomerate)
	Devonian 345 MYA — first amphibians appear	Ouray (limestone)
	Cambrian 500 MYA — complex marine invertebrates appear	Tonto (mixed rock)
		granite/schist

PRECAMBRIAN ERA 570+ MYA

112